FOOTBALL LINEMEN

The Center, Guard, Tackle & Ends

The images in this volume were scanned from
original sources in

The Lost Century of Sports Collection

and may not be reproduced in any form
without prior written permission.

ISBN-10: 1466204745
ISBN-13: 978-1466204744

Library of Congress Control Number: 2011936112

Printed in the United States of America

The Lost Century of Sports Collection

www.LostCentury.com

FOOTB✭LL LINEMEN

The CENTER, GUARD, TACKLE & ENDS

Written Over a Century Ago by

3 Hall of Fame Coaches

and the Man Who Invented the Flying Wedge

| WALTER CAMP | AMOS ALONZO STAGG |
| LORIN F. DELAND | HENRY L. WILLIAMS |

This volume contains the chapters about linemen from the
following three classic books:

AMERICAN FOOTBALL

By **Walter Camp**

Harper & Brothers, Franklin Square
New York, **1891**

A Scientific and Practical Treatise on AMERICAN FOOTBALL for Schools and Colleges

By **A. Alonzo Stagg**
and **Henry L. Williams**

Press of The Case, Lockwood & Brainard
Company, Hartford, Conn., **1893**

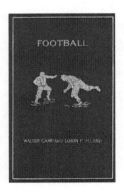

FOOTBALL

By **Walter Camp** and
Lorin F. Deland

Houghton, Mifflin and Company
The Riverside Press, Cambridge
Boston and New York, **1896**

CONTENTS

THE AUTHORS

 **WALTER CAMP** (1859-1925) was the first football coach and literally wrote the football rule book. He was Yale's best player and captain in the 1870's when the sport was played under Rugby rules. As the most prominent member of the football rules committee in the 1880's, Camp introduced the line of scrimmage, the scoring system, the series of downs to retain the ball, and other fundamental features of the game. He was widely-known as "the Father of American Football" by the time these books were published. Many of his former players became pioneering coaches at colleges nationwide. Camp was a prolific writer and America's most admired sports authority.

 **AMOS ALONZO STAGG** (1862-1965) was a famous player for Walter Camp at Yale and was named to the first All-American team in 1889. In 1892 the University of Chicago hired Stagg as the nation's first athletic director and football coach with faculty status. The diagrammed plays in his book became templates for innovative coaches to design their own plays. "The Grand Old Man of Football" was named Coach of the Year at age 81, and retired from coaching at age 97 with 314 career victories. Stagg was a standout pitcher in college and played in the first public basketball game in 1892. He is a member of both the football and basketball Hall of Fame.

 **HENRY L. WILLIAMS** (1869-1931) was Stagg's teammate on Walter Camp's Yale squad. In 1891 he invented the "tackle-back" formation, coached West Point to its first victory against Annapolis, and set the world record in the 120 yard high hurdles. He later became the head football coach at the University of Minnesota for 22 years, during which he also maintained a medical practice. Dr. Williams was an influential member of the rules committee and an early proponent of the forward pass. Williams was inducted into the College Football Hall of Fame in the inaugural class of 1951, along with Camp and Stagg.

 **LORIN F. DELAND** (1855-1917) was a military historian who never played football, or even attended a game, until he was in his mid-thirties. Within two years he was Harvard's head coach and recognized as a football genius. Deland analyzed the American sport as if it were a battlefield and devised plays based on military tactics, including the fabled "flying wedge," which he unveiled in a game against Walter Camp in 1892. The two rival coaches united in 1896 to write their comprehensive study of the sport.

INTRODUCTION

This volume contains the chapters about linemen from the first three major books ever written about modern football, by three Hall of Fame coaches and the man who invented the flying wedge:

American Football, by Walter Camp (1891)

A Scientific and Practical Treatise on American Football for Schools and Colleges, by Amos Alonzo Stagg and Henry L. Williams (1893).

Football, by Walter Camp and Lorin F. Deland (1896).

The original books were written during an era when players played the entire game without substitution. As a result, the descriptions of player positions mingled the responsibilities of what are now three separate and specialized offensive, defensive, and special teams platoons.

Offensive backs were also defensive backs, punters, place-kickers, and kick-returners. The fullback was the defensive safety and primary kicker. The quarterback played a linebacker position ("rush line back") on defense.

Linemen (also called "forwards" and "rushers") likewise played both offense and defense. The offensive tackle was sometimes used as a ball-carrier. This confusion is clarified in this updated volume which separates and categorizes the responsibilities into offensive and defensive platoons.

"In touch" refers to out of bounds. Playing the ball "from a fair" was the method of putting the ball in play from out of bounds, before hashmarks were devised.

The images in this volume were originally published in newspapers and magazines from 1857 to 1900. Sources and captions are shown in the List of Illustrations.

The Lost Century of Sports Collection publishes rare works from America's sporting heritage. Volumes include *The Lost Century of American Football*, *The American Football Trilogy*, *The First Decade of Women's Basketball*, and *Daughters of the Lost Century*.

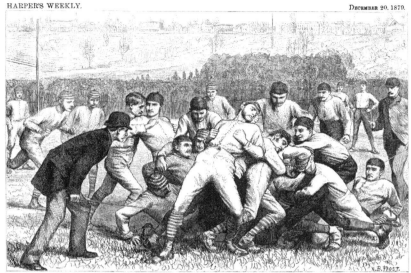

HARPER'S WEEKLY. DECEMBER 20, 1870.

FOOT-BALL MATCH BETWEEN YALE AND PRINCETON, NOVEMBER 27.—Drawn by A. B. Frost.

THE CENTER

WALTER CAMP:

If any old players come back to help the team in the way of coaching, and among them are some center rushers, they can do no better work than by donning a uniform and playing against the "'Varsity" center.

A coach should see to it that his center has a variety of men to face, some big, some tricky, some ugly. Practical experience has taught football coaches that none but a thoroughly self-controlled man can make a success in football in any position, while in this particular one his disposition should be of the most equable nature. The man who may be selected to fill the important position of center-rush must be a man of sense and strength. Brain and brawn are here at their highest premium. But there is another element of character without which both will be overthrown, and that is patience. He will be called upon to face all kinds of petty annoyances, for his opponents will endeavor to make his play as difficult as possible; and never must he allow himself for one instant to lose sight of the fact that his entire attention must be devoted to his play, and none of it distracted by personal feeling.

Moreover, while he must be able to play the ball quickly when called upon, he can never afford to be hurried by his opponents.

With the present excellent rulings of umpires regarding interference with the ball before it is snapped, much of the most harassing kicking of the ball from under his hand has been stopped; but, for all that, he is indeed a lucky center who does not feel the ball knocked out from under his grasp several times during a game.

In addition to this, every man who breaks through gives him a rub. Sometimes these knocks are intentional, often they are given purely by accident, and the latter are by no means the lightest. Then, too, a man is pushed into the snap-back just as the ball goes.

It may be his own guard, but the blow hurts just as much; and a center who is not amiable under such treatment soon loses his head and forgets that he should care for nothing except to accomplish gains for his own side. The object of placing so much stress upon this qualification is to impress upon a coach the almost inestimable value of the quality of patience in any men he may be trying for this position. He can never say too much about it.

As regards the duties of the place, they differ from those of any other position in the line on account of the constant presence at that spot of the ball.

The center is either playing the ball himself or watching his antagonist play the ball at every down; so that while he has all the other duties of a forward to execute, he has the special work besides.

Here is the weakness of so many centers. They are snap-backs only or forwards only, the former being by all odds the more common. A good critical coach of experience will see nine out of every ten men whom he may watch in this position playing through day after day with no more idea of doing any forward work than if they were referees.

Putting the ball in play at the right time, and properly, is a great achievement, but it does not free the center-rush from all other obligations. He must protect his quarter; he must aid in making openings, and perform any interference that may be possible, as well as always assisting a runner of his own side with weight or protection. He must always get down the field under a kick, for it is by no means unusual for him to have the best opportunity in these days when end rushers are so carefully watched.

HARPER'S WEEKLY.   AUGUST 1, 1857.

THE MATCH BETWEEN SOPHS AND FRESHMEN.

STAGG & WILLIAMS:

The prevailing idea in time past has been that the largest and heaviest man who could be procured should be used for the center-rusher, or snapback of the eleven. So universal has this idea become that it has long been a common joke to say of an especially large and stout person: "He would make a good center-rusher." Every new team formed, as a rule, selects the center according to this axiomatic fallacy. It is easy to see how this principle of selection became established under the old pushing style of game, and it still should hold sway, provided it brings with the selection certain qualities of mind, and certain physical capacities, which will enable the center to be one of the most active and effective agents on the field.

The ideal center will be one who is swift of foot in addition to his other powers. He should be a large man, not a ponderous man, unless he is quick and strong.

He should be especially strong in his legs and back, for he must stand steadily on his feet against the continuous pushing and wrestling which he receives, directly from the opponents, and incidentally from the guards on either side of him. If he is easily moved, or toppled over, he will be likely now and then to snap the ball poorly, thus making the quarter-back uneasy and flurried in handling it. Steadiness is a most necessary part of the center's work and it cannot well be overlooked in the selection of a man to fill that position.

Further, as in every position on the eleven endurance is a prime requisite, so is it in this. More of it is needed, however, than in most others, because the work is much harder.

No short-winded, fat man can long stand the hard work of that position, if he does his duty.

Not only is great physical labor required of the center, but he must also be constantly subjected to knocks and bruises from the plunging and tearing of the rushers and half-backs as they try to break through the line. No man, therefore, can play in this position who is not physically courageous, and who is not able to rise to his work after each assault with new grit and determination.

He should be a man who is cool and collected at all times; combative, but never losing control of his temper; one who endures worrying without being rattled by it; one who never gives up and is bound to conquer.

Nowhere in the line is there need for such steadiness as in the center. From him every play starts, in a scrimmage, and a little unsteadiness on his part will be likely to make havoc with the quarter-back's work, and hence with the offensive play of the whole team.

Nothing can be more fatal to quick and steady play, for it is sure to produce hesitancy in action in some of the players, with hurried action in others. The center occupies a unique position on the eleven in that he starts the play after each down, and is the only member of the team who cannot run with the ball from a scrimmage, because it is impossible to make him a third man advantageously. His work, therefore, is limited in that particular.

By reason, also, of his having to protect the quarter-back after he snaps the ball, and because he is invariably entangled with the opponents, it is impossible for him to become a valuable running interferer. What work in interference he is able to do is limited to blocking the opponents from breaking through the line, or running behind their own line to head off the runner with the ball at one side.

Possibly, when very clever and swift, he may be able to cut across the field to interfere with a half-back or the full-back.

The center should make a practice of doing this latter work on every play around the end, and on every play between the tackle and end. Perhaps he may not be able to get ahead of the runner, but he will be of valuable assistance by checking some of the opponents from running behind their line and tackling him.

Now and then, also, he will be able to get ahead of the runner and go down the field with him.

From these statements it might appear that it did not matter especially whether the center rusher was a slow runner or not, and that emphasis should be laid on his possessing size and weight, which are understood as necessary to the proper filling of that position. The truth is, that while a slow runner, if he has cleverness for that position and is strong and weighty, will be able to do fairly well as a center, he cannot begin to be as serviceable to his team as if he were also a fast runner.

Granting that a fast runner will not be able to do much interfering, or running with the ball, he will still be able to use his speed most helpfully in breaking through the line to tackle; in crossing over to one side to head off a runner; or in going down the field on a kick. Furthermore, his speed will be most helpful in playing a quick game, because he is thus able to follow the ball so closely that there will be no delay in putting it in play. This is a most important point in the center's play.

He must be on hand to receive the ball the instant it is down. It is impossible to play a quick game where the center lags, or to prevent one on the part of the opponents. When there are not many large men who are fast runners it is better, perhaps, to place the speedy man in the position of guard and take a slower man for center.

There are various ways for the center to handle his man and get him out of his way. He may plunge forward at the instant he snaps the ball, carrying his opponent before him, he may lift him to one side or the other, according to the play called for and the position of the opponent; he may fall on him if he is down too low; or he may get under him and lift him in the air, if his opponent reaches over him. In any one of these methods, the opportune moment must be seized like a flash and the action be quick and powerful. A slow, strong movement will never succeed. Long and faithful practice is necessary before the center can acquire this quickness and power.

In his eagerness to take advantage of his opponent, he must never fail to wait for the quarter-back's signal before snapping the ball. A little forgetfulness on this point might prove disastrous.

CAMP & DELAND:

The Centre. *More General Activity.* Having thus covered the places on both sides, we should complete the discussion of the duties of the linesmen by a description of the work of the centre. He, like the guard, is a man of weight. But, while in the case of the guard we need, or rather expect, more general activity in breaking through, in the case of the centre we require more steadiness. For it is indispensable to the success of any play that the ball be snapped back properly to the quarter, and that uniformity of movement be preserved at this point in the play.

How to Stand. A centre must be strong on his legs, and must devote a great deal of practice to securing a good poise. The method of standing with both feet nearly on a line is preferable to placing one foot back farther than the other for a brace, although a centre who can stand in the former way may occasionally rest himself or bother his opponents by a change.

Special Instructions for Blocking by the Centre-Rush. The problem of the centre-rush on the offense has been rendered much simpler by the recent legislation which forbids the opposing centre from interfering with the ball until it is put in play. Before this law was enacted, the blocking of the centre-rush was one of the most important features in the play of the line; but having now the exclusive control of the ball until it is snapped, his difficulties are greatly lessened.

There are various ways for the centre to block his man after he has put the ball in play. Of course, he knows the exact instant when the ball is to go back, and in this respect he has a great advantage over any other man in the rush-line. He can plunge forward into his opponent on the instant that he snaps the ball, gaining a foot or more by the very force of his plunge; or, if his opponent is down too low, he may fall on him. Beside this, he can frequently lift him to one side or the other, and in any event he has little difficulty in protecting the quarter, so far as interference from the opposing centre is concerned.

As for the position of his feet, it is a great advantage if he can keep his feet on a line, neither foot being in advance of the other. It is possible to take such a position, and be firmly braced in all directions.

If, however, the centre finds it difficult to thus brace himself, let him take the position which the tackle would assume. This might be described as almost identical with the position of a sprinter "on the mark." The body bends at the knees and hips; and the support being on the toes, with the joints very springy, the position is altogether a very comfortable one to maintain; although it can easily be proved that the position first recommended for the centre is by far the better one to adopt.

THE SNAP

WALTER CAMP:

It is no child's play to hold a ball out at arm's length on the ground in front of one and roll it back so that it passes between one's feet, and still preserve a good balance in spite of a sudden push of a hundred-and-eighty-pound opponent. But that is just what a center has to do every time the ball is down and belongs to his side.

The details of the special work of the center are many, and thorough knowledge of them can only come from experience. During his early progress a new snap-back usually sends the ball against his own legs, or, if he manages to keep them out of the way, is upset by his opponent for his pains.

The first thing to teach a center is to stand on his feet against any amount of jostling. Then he must learn to keep possession of the ball until ready to play it. Both of these acquirements take practice. The most finished and experienced centers have a way of playing the ball just as they are half straightening as though to meet a charge from in front. This insures their not being pushed over on to the quarter, and yet does not cause them to lean so far forward as to be pitched on their noses by a little assistance from the opposing center.

When a man stands so as to prevent a push in the chest from upsetting him, he naturally puts one foot back some distance as a support. When a center does this he is apt to put that foot and leg in the path of the ball.

A second objection to this way of standing is, that the center does not offer nearly as much opposition to any one attempting to pass as he does when he stands more squarely faced about with a good spread of the legs.

As to holding the ball, some centers prefer to take it by the end, while others roll it on its side. It can be made to rise for the quarter if sent on end, whereas if played upon its side it lies closer to the ground. The quarter's

preference has, therefore, something to do with it.

It requires longer practice and more skill to play the ball on its end, but it permits an umpire to see more clearly whether the ball be actually put in play by the snap-back or played for him by the surreptitious kick of the opponent. It has also the advantage of sending the ball more narrowly upon a line, so that its course is less likely to be altered than when rolled upon its side.

While the snap-back is seldom held to the very strictest conformity to the rule about being on side when he puts the ball in play, it is necessary for him to practice with a view to this particular, because he is liable to be obliged to conform every time if the opponents insist. The reason for carelessness in this respect is, there is no penalty for infringement except being obliged to return to the spot and put the ball in play properly. A certain laxity, therefore, is granted rather than to cause delays. But, as stated above, a center must be able to put the ball in play when fairly on side, and must live up to this with some moderate degree of regularity, or else the umpire will call an off side and bring him back.

A center ought to practice putting the ball in play with either hand until he is fairly proficient with his left as well as his right.

Not that he should use his hands alternately in a game, but that an injury to his right hand need not necessarily throw him out of the game. It is by no means an unrecognized fact that the greater amount of experience possessed by the regular center is so valuable as to make it policy to keep him in his place so long as his legs are good, even though a hand be injured, rather than to replace him by the substitute with whose methods the quarter-back is not so familiar.

STAGG & WILLIAMS:

A good referee will see to it that the ball is snapped each time from the proper spot. In assuming his position for a scrimmage, the center may follow either of two methods of standing, when snapping the ball: one, where one foot is placed back for a brace, the ball being snapped between the legs and a little to one side; the other, where both feet are widely spread to interfere with opponents, as they attempt to break through, and to avoid getting into the way of the ball which can be snapped straight back.

Where the first position is followed, the center should be able to work equally well with either foot forward, in order to secure certain advantages in handling his opponent.

The center-rusher should make a study of the best way of snapping the ball back, and then hold it the same way every time. He should confer with the quarter-back on this point, as the latter is to handle the ball, and it may be easier to take it when snapped in a particular way.

There are two methods followed in snapping the ball: one, in which the ball is held on the small end and sent back swiftly with little effort, in such a way that the quarter-back catches it in the air all ready to pass; the other, where the ball is laid on its side and rolled along

the ground to the point where it is stopped by the quarter-back and then picked up in very good position for passing.

This latter method is more generally used because it does not require as delicate work on the part of the center in giving the snap; but speed is sacrificed by it and there is greater liability that the ball shall be deflected from its course by touching the legs.

It would be well for the center to learn to use either hand in snapping, for it will often prove an advantage. The center-rusher will do well to make a study of snapping the ball by both methods of standing, and by both ways of holding it until he settles on the one

best suited to him. He should then practice this against an opponent until he is able to stand firmly on his feet and send the ball back accurately, at a uniform rate of speed each time. In case the ball is placed on end, it is better to have it lean toward the opposing center at an angle of about sixty degrees. It can be held more firmly in this position and can also be sent back more swiftly, with a bound into the air. Care must be taken not to send the ball too swiftly.

While the center is practicing to secure steadiness, accuracy, and uniformity in snapping the ball, he should likewise practice getting his opponent out of the way.

In putting the ball in play, the center has the advantage of being able to select the time to snap and he can choose it to meet his own purpose. Besides, he knows the exact instant when he intends to send the ball back and can get the start of his opponent.

The center, therefore, is master of the situation when he has the ball. It is for these reasons that he can frequently be down the field on a kick as soon as the ends, and yet not expose the full-back to great danger in having the ball stopped.

DEFENSIVE CENTER

WALTER CAMP:

When the opponents have the ball, he must not be content with seeing that the opponent does not roll it to a

guard, but must also see that there is no short, tricky passing in the scrimmage. Then he must be as ready as either guard to meet, stop, or turn a wedge. He must make openings for his comrades to get through, even when he himself may be blocked, and always be ready to reach out or throw himself before a coming runner to check the advance.

STAGG & WILLIAMS:

The center can be a most valuable man in defensive play if he understands his position. Whenever he succeeds in getting through he will be a strong obstacle to all dashes between himself and the guards, and he will sometimes be able to interfere with the quarter-back's pass.

By giving his opponents a quick pull forward or to one side at the instant the latter snaps the ball; by lifting him suddenly backward; or by grasping his arm, the center can frequently break through more quickly than either guard or tackle.

Another way in which the center may play on the defense is to spend all his energy for a moment in getting his opponent out of his way and then spring at the runner. In this case the center must throw off his opponent quickly, and not allow himself to be carried backward. At the same time he must not attempt to break through the line. When the play is around the end, or even at the tackle, the center should move quickly from his position and pass around behind his own line to meet and tackle the runner.

When the opposite side is about to kick, the center should do his utmost to break through the line and stop it; but sometimes it may be better instead to make an opening for the quarter-back.

He is helped in doing this, by the opposite center himself, as he plunges forward to block him. In such a case a good opening can be made for the quarter-back, if the center will place himself in front of his opponent a little to one side, and then pull the latter forward to the right or left. The guard at the side on which the opening is made should know of this plan so that he may not spoil it, either by pushing his opponent in the path or by getting in the way himself.

If there is danger of his doing this, it will be better for him to help enlarge the opening for the quarter-back.

On the defensive the center may play a little to one side or the other of his opponent, or directly in front, to suit the situation.

It is most unwise for the center to assume the same position every time, for by so doing he gives the opposite center only one problem to work out and that one probably the same each time.

Where the center takes an extreme side position, unless he does it just before the ball is snapped, he gives the captain of the other eleven a fine chance to call for a play which will take advantage of the situation.

There is abundant opportunity for the display of headwork in outwitting the opposing center in breaking through the line. The line is so compact at this point that it is not an easy task to slip by, especially as the opposing center is watching to take his man at a disadvantage.

Various methods are resorted to in breaking through the line. Sometimes the center, acting on the defense, is thrown head foremost to the ground by a quick, hard pull, the attacking center stepping aside or over him as he falls.

He may also be turned sidewise just enough to slip past him, or he may be lifted back perhaps into the face of the runner. The most common method employed by the center in getting through is to catch the arm of the opponent on the side on which it is desired to go through, give it a jerk, and dash into the opening.

The center in defense must insist on the ball being down where it belongs. Some center-rushers have a way of moving the ball forward several inches further than it should be. There is no occasion for generosity under such circumstances, and the center must feel that it is his duty to stand up for the rights of his team by constantly guarding against any infringement of this kind.

On the other hand, a constant bickering over an inch or two of ground may be made of such importance that the game is interfered with and delayed to such an extent that a much greater gain would have resulted were the ball put in play the instant the signal called for it.

It is always the duty of the center-rusher to keep close to the opponent who brings the ball in from the side line, in order to protect the rights of his team.

Likewise, it is well to "pace in" the opponent who brings the ball to the twenty-five yard line, in order to prevent a quick play being made when his own side are not in position. The guards assist him in this.

CAMP & DELAND:

Defensive Play. In defensive work, that is, when the opponents have the ball, he should endeavor, while protecting the centre openings, to throw his opposing snap-back over on to his quarter at times, and he should also keep him very nervous about the openings. He, the centre, may go through himself, or he may help a guard through, or he may make an opening for his quarter to get through.

Like all line men, he should have a variety of methods for accomplishing his object, and should seldom do the thing twice in the same way.

INTERCOLLEGIATE FOOT-BALL—"DOWN!"—DRAWN BY C. D. GIBSON.

THE GUARDS

WALTER CAMP:

The position of guard, while it requires less agility than that of tackle, can never be satisfactorily filled by a man who is slow.

Many a coach makes this mistake and fails to see his error until too late to correct it. I remember once seeing upon a minor team a guard who weighed at least 190 pounds replaced by a man of 155, and the latter actually filled the position–greatly to my astonishment, I confess–in excellent fashion.

This does not at all go to prove that weight is of no value in a guard. On the contrary, it is a quality especially to be desired, and if one can find a heavy man who is not slow he is the choice by all means.

But weight must be given work to do, and that work demands practice, and slowness of execution cannot be tolerated. At the outset the coach must impress this fact upon the guards, and insist upon their doing their work quickly. It is really wonderful how much better the effect of that work will prove to be when performed with a snap and dash that are not difficult to acquire.

STAGG & WILLIAMS:

The main work of the guards may be summed up as blocking, that is, guarding: making openings for the passage of the runner whenever certain signals are given; running behind the line to interfere for the man with the ball; running with the ball occasionally; breaking through the opposing line to interfere with the quarter-back in passing the ball; and tackling the runner or stopping a kick.

The guards and the center have the most laborious work on the eleven, if they do their duty, for they practically have no respite from hard work. They must bear the brunt of the heavy plunging of their opponents

though the center, and at the same time struggle to break through the opposing line, which is doing its utmost to prevent them. They must do this without a let-up just as long as the other side has the ball, and, moreover, in that part of the line which is most compact.

Then, when their own side has the ball, they are expected to use their strength and wits from the moment the ball is put in play until it is again down, in blocking, making openings, and in interfering for the player who is attempting to run. Further, they have little time to catch their wind, for almost the first point which should be drummed into them by the captain or coach is to be always on hand the moment the ball is down, to make or prevent a quick play. It can be truly said that no team is well trained until the center part of the eleven, as indeed the whole team, is prompt on this point.

While the guards have all this hard work, they seldom have a chance to distinguish themselves, either by a run, a clean tackle, or a fine interference which is apparent to the untrained eye of the spectator.

On the other hand, it does not take much yielding at the center to bring forth criticism that that part of the line is weak. On account of the nature of their work, the guards should be large and powerful, like the center.

It is even more necessary that they should be quick, agile, and swift, than the center, because the guards should always go through the line when the opponents have the ball. On their success in doing this largely depends the strength or weakness of the team's defense.

CAMP & DELAND:

The Guard. *Steady and Powerful.* The guard is a peculiar type of man. He is apt to carry with his added pounds an amount of laziness and good-natured carelessness that requires all the coaching possible to eradicate.

He ought to be a powerful fellow in legs, body, and arms. The more quickness he has with these the better; but he must, to play the modern game, be heavy. His duties on defense lie in assisting the tackle, and in protecting the opening between himself and tackle, as well as between himself and centre.

He ought to plow through hard and low, but with enough swing to insure stopping any man trying to come through outside him.

COLLEGE PLAYERS AT FOOT-BALL—"A TACKLE AND BALL-DOWN."—Drawn by Frederic Remington

OFFENSIVE GUARD

WALTER CAMP:

When his own side have the ball the guard must block sharply until the quarter has time for receiving the ball, and, at any rate, beginning the motion of the pass. It is safer, in the case of inexperienced guards, to tell them to block until the quarter has time to get rid of the ball.

The distinction is this: that an experienced guard sometimes likes to gain just that second of time between the beginning of the pass and the completion of the swing, and utilize it in getting down the field or making an opening. So accustomed does he become to measuring the time correctly that he will let the opponent through just too late to reach the quarter, although it seems a very close call. It is not safe to let green guards attempt anything so close. They must be taught to block securely until the ball is on its way to the runner or kicker.

The blocking of a guard is much less exacting in its requirements than that of the tackle. Not that he must not block with equal certainty, but the act requires no such covering of two men as often happens in the case of a tackle.

The guard forms closely towards the center, and then follows his man out if he moves out, but only as far as he can go, and still be absolutely certain that the opponent cannot pass between him and the snap-back. To be drawn or coaxed out far enough to admit of an opponent's going through the center shows woeful ignorance in any guard.

When blocking for a run, of course much depends upon where the opening is to be made, and a guard must be governed accordingly. The method itself is, again, different in the guard from that exhibited in the tackle.

A guard may not move about so freely and must face his man more squarely than a tackle, for the guard must protect the quarter first, while the tackle considers the half only. If a guard allows his opponent to get a fair lunge with outstretched arm over or past his shoulder, he may reach the quarter's arm even though his body is checked, while such a reach at the point in the line occupied by the tackle would be of no value whatever.

Previous to the snap-back's playing the ball it is the duty of the guards to see that their individual opponents do not succeed in either kicking the ball out from the snap-back's hand or otherwise interfering with his play.

This is quite an important feature, and a center should always feel that he has upon either hand a steady and wide-awake assistant, who will neither be caught napping nor allow any unfair advantage to be taken of him.

The guard should bear in mind one fact, however, and that most clearly. It is that squabbling and general pushing about are far more liable to disconcert his own center and quarter than to interfere with the work of the opponents.

CAMP JOHNSON, NEAR WINCHESTER, VIRGINIA—THE FIRST MARYLAND REGIMENT PLAYING FOOT-BALL BEFORE EVENING PARADE.

STAGG & WILLIAMS:

The position of the guard varies slightly in defense and offense. In offense the first thought must be to protect the quarter-back until he has passed the ball; his next to block his man long enough to prevent him from reaching the runner. His third thought, which may also influence the way he stands while he attends to the former work, is to make the opening if the play is in his quarter. His fourth thought, which will be influenced by his first and second, is to get in his interference ahead of the runner when practicable, or follow him as closely as possible and do what he can to assist.

In fulfilling all these duties he will be limited in his freedom of movement. He cannot stand too far from the center rusher, and he may be compelled to stand shoulder to shoulder with him. Further, he will have to assume a position which best enables him to carry out his duties. It may be well for him to stand with both feet on a line, or it may be better to have one or the other foot behind, according to his purpose.

It is nearly always better for him to bend forward, or even to get down very low if his opponent tries to get under him. The bent-over position is better for meeting attacks, because the weight is well forward and low down and the body is better braced and not so much exposed to effective handling. In this position, also, one can move forward better for making an opening.

When the guard runs around to interfere, he should place himself so that he can get away quickly and not "give the play away." If the guard is to run around in order to interfere by getting ahead of the runners, the quickest possible start is necessary. There must be no delay whatever, even when the guard is a fast runner, or else the runner with the ball will have to slow up so much that he cannot make the play. Whenever the guard runs around to interfere or to run with the ball, the tackle should keep the opposing guard from following him. The guard can sometimes do this himself by pushing his opponent back just as he starts, but it must be done in such a way that it will not delay him.

"Block hard" has come to be one of the axioms of the game. In blocking the legs should usually be spread widely apart. They should not be spread so much, however, that the guard will not be able to move quickly whenever his opponent shifts his position. In blocking, as in breaking through the line, the guard should try hard to get his power into action before his opponent. This can be best done by a shoulder check.

The general position of the guard must be determined by the play in hand and the way the opponent stands. He may be forced to move out a little because his opponent does so, but he must be careful that the opening between him and the center is not occupied by the quarter-back or some other free player, in which case the tackle will sometimes be obliged to step in and take the opposing guard. Neither the guard nor any other rusher except the center should ever take a fixed position in standing.

The quarter-back, being so near to the guards, is in imminent danger in case of weak blocking, and he can little afford the loss of a fraction of a second in handling the ball, much less a fumble. Under these circumstances, if a fumble occurs, the quarter-back must always fall on the ball and not run any risks of losing it. Furthermore in weak blocking, the runner has little chance on a dash into the line, for in place of an opening he finds an opponent.

The guard has an advantage over the center in making an opening for the runner in only one particular, and that is that he is freer to move in his position. The center rusher is largely dependent on the position which his opponent takes in standing to help him out in this matter, since he cannot move his relative position from the opposing center more than the latter allows; but he can often influence that position to suit his own purpose.

By clever generalship and strategy he may be able to induce his opponent to do the very thing he needs to help him out in his play. Some of the ways of handling an opponent are given in the description of the duties of the center rusher.

Long-legged guards, as a rule, find it easier to take a long step backward with the foot next the center, and use that as a purchase from which to circle around the quarter-back. Some guards prefer to take three or four short, quick steps in making the turn around the quarter-back.

Any way which will enable the guard to get under headway most quickly is the method which should be used. It will be easy for the quarter-back to place the ball in the guard's hands, and it will probably be better for him to carry it under the arm away from the center.

When the guard is going to run with the ball he should take a position which will enable him to get away from his opponent quickly, but he should not make his intentions evident. For this reason it is better for the guard, as well as for the tackle, not to take a set position until the signal is given; but if one is taken, let it be such that it would not make it necessary to change in order to run with the ball. The one who is to run with the ball should seek in every way to conceal the purpose of the play. The guard is in the most difficult position from which to get under headway in order to run with the ball.

As commonly played, the guard swings round the quarter-back and dives into an opening between the tackle and guard on the other side of the center. The very beginning of his run is the most difficult part. He cannot run fast from his position, for he has only a step or two to make before he must turn sharply around the quarter-back and run in almost an opposite direction. If he runs back too far he will be tackled before he reaches the line, and if he turns in closely, he is likely to run against his own men as they are struggling with their opponents.

It needs, therefore, careful judgment and a great deal of practice to be able run well from this position.

LINING UP.

CAMP & DELAND:

A Protection on Offense. On the offense, that is, when his side has possession of the ball, it is his duty to see that the quarter-back is thoroughly protected. That is his first duty, and until he has accomplished that he should attempt nothing else.

There is no more fatal blunder than that of allowing the quarter to be interfered with. But after that duty is performed, he has, in the running game, to make openings for plays on his own side the line, and to get out into the interference in plays over on the far side. Like the tackle, he may also be used to run with the ball, both from his position and by dropping back.

Special Instructions for Blocking by a Guard. A guard in blocking has several duties to perform, and we will mention these duties in the order of their importance, for this is the order in which they should be in his mind, and in which they should receive his attention.

His first duty is to protect his centre in making the snap, and his quarter in securing the ball and making the pass; his second is the necessity of blocking his opponent long enough to prevent him from reaching the runner; next, the making an opening on either side of his position in the line; and lastly comes the necessity of getting into the interference himself as quickly and as strongly as possible.

It follows, naturally, that in performing all these various duties he will be somewhat limited in his freedom of movement, and his position must necessarily be more or less controlled by the exigencies of the occasion.

In general, the guard should stand with his feet well spread apart. It is a safe rule to keep the legs as far apart as possible, up to the limit of not hindering his quickness and activity. The advantage is always with the man who can earliest put his power into action.

A very effective method of blocking for a guard is what is commonly known as the shoulder-check, which consists in meeting an opponent strongly on the upper part of his hips with the outside shoulder.

It must be borne in mind that the blocking of the guard is of greater importance than the work of any other man in the line, for his close proximity to the quarter-back makes weak blocking here a serious menace to the safety of the pass. The guard should be careful not to allow his opponent to draw him too far from his own centre. He may follow his opponent out a little, but the limit of safety in this direction is quickly reached.

The guard of all other players must learn long blocking, for this is the method which he must always employ when a kick is ordered. In general, no set rules need be laid down for the guard as to the placing of his feet; the better position, if he can take it, is to stand with both feet on a line; this will be hard to acquire and somewhat painful at first, but the advantages of such a position repay his efforts. All his blocking should be done with his body very low bent fairly well forward. In this position he can be better braced, and not so much exposed to the rough handling of an opponent.

The guard's position in blocking will, of course, be different if he is himself to run with the ball. For this, it is necessary that he should get away free and clear from his opponent the instant the snap is made. He can sometimes contrive to strike his opponent in the chest, and then let the very force of his push or blow be his own impetus in the opposite direction. In any case, there must not be a moment's delay in getting clear.

Whatever method will get the guard under headway in the shortest order will be the proper method to use.

DEFENSIVE GUARD

STAGG & WILLIAMS:

On the defensive much depends on strong blocking by the guards, for weak blocking is fatal at the center of the line. The chief point in defensive play is to tackle the runner before he reaches the line, and the guards are large factors in doing this.

Unless this is done, the ball can be steadily carried down the field when not lost by a fumble, for any team is able to gain five yards in three consecutive trials when the runner is allowed to reach the line each time before being tackled. Any means, therefore, which the guards can employ to interfere with the quarter-back before he has passed the ball, or the runner before he has reached the line, should certainly be used. All the strategy and tricks known in wrestling which can be applied to the situation should be eagerly sought and practiced.

The great point to remember is to apply the power quickly and hard, to summon all the strength for the initial effort, and to work desperately until free from interference. Only by doing this can the guards hope to break through and secure the quarter-back or runner behind the line.

Slow pushing, however powerful, will accomplish little. If held in check until the runner and the pushers strike the line it is only a question of how many yards the runner will gain before the mass breaks and falls forward.

In applying his power the guard, as well as his companion rushers, has an immense advantage in being permitted to use his hands and arms freely in getting his opponent out of the way. This enables  him to put into practice all the skill he possesses in handling an opponent who is allowed to block only with the body.

The guard also has another advantage in being free to move whenever he pleases, but he must remember that the opening for the runner may be made on either side of him and be careful not to give his opponent help in making it.

It assists the guard greatly in breaking through if the tackle draws out the opposing line as much as is wise in a good defense. This separation should be wide enough to allow the players in defense to break through easily without interfering with each other.

It is also usually helpful in breaking through to be restless, but cautious at the same time, in order not to give the opponent an advantage.

The guards and the tackles especially should watch for signs which shall indicate what the play will be, and then go through the line as low as possible for a tackle. They should break through to the right or left of their opponents as seems best at the moment. In order to break through quickly they must have their eyes on the ball when it is snapped and spring forward the instant it is put in play. Quick glances may be cast at the opponents while still constantly watching the ball. The guards, with the center, are usually called upon to meet the heavy charges in the opening plays from the center of the field. These, as a rule, come in the form of wedges.

Two points should be carefully regarded by these center men in attacking a wedge; first, to approach the wedge with the body bent in a position for the greatest power and for meeting the wedge down low; second, to focus on the mass in such a way that it cannot break through between them without being separated, and so giving the guards a chance to tackle the runner.

In doing this it should be the aim to focus as nearly as possible upon the point of the wedge, in order to check its advance and throw the forwards back on the runner.

LINE UP

The runner will then be forced to come out, if he has not already become entangled in the mass. In making the attack the guards and center should run with dash and determination, at the same time watching closely for the runner and trying hard to tackle him.

Two successful ways of attacking a wedge have been originated. One member of the center trio will sometimes jump over the heads of the forwards and try to fall on the runner and thus secure him, or he will hurl himself headlong at the feet of the oncoming wedge and cause it to trip over him. To make either one of these attacks well the player must be perfectly fearless, and should also use good judgment. In the former case the player must time his jump and not land short of the runner, or he will be pushed quickly to the ground or carried along on the heads of the forwards; neither must he jump so far over that he will miss his man.

If he throws himself in front of the wedge he should not do it too soon, lest the wedge will be able to avoid or step over him. When a wedge is formed in the line on a scrimmage the guards and center must be sure to get low, or they will be carried along before it. The point of the wedge must be held in check. In resisting the attack of a revolving wedge the guards should separate slightly from the center and join with the tackle in trying to penetrate the mass to secure the runner.

This should be done in such a way that the defense shall not be weakened. Care should also be taken by the side of the line away from which the wedge revolves not to add impetus to it by pushing too far.

WALTER CAMP:

To continue with the work of the guard when the opponents are about to attempt a run. One of the most important features of the play in this position is to guard against small wedges. If a guard simply stands still and straight he will be swept over like a wisp of straw by any well-executed wedge play directed at him. An experienced man knows this, and his chief thought

December 7, 1889.

"LINING UP."

is how to avoid it, and how, first, to prevent the formation; second, to alter the direction, and, finally, to stop the progress, of this terror of center work, the small wedge.

There are as many ways of accomplishing these results as of performing the duties of tackle or end, and it rests with the individual player to study them out.

To prevent the formation of small wedges, the most successful method is that of sudden and, if possible, disconcerting movements. Jostling, so far as it is allowed, sudden change of position, a pretended charge–all these tend to break up the close formation.

Once formed and started, the change of direction is usually the most disarranging play possible; but this  should not be attempted by the player or players opposite the point of the wedge.

At that spot the proper play is to check the advance, even temporarily; for the advance once checked, the wedge may be swung from the side so as to take off the pressure from behind. So it is the men at the side who must endeavor to turn the wedge and take off this pressure.

Without the actual formation upon the field it is difficult to fully explain this turning of the wedge; but if the principle of the defense be borne in mind, it will not be found so hard to understand. Check the peak even for a moment, and get the weight off from behind as speedily as possible.

The men who are pushing must necessarily act blindly; and if their force is not directly upon the men at the point of the V, they pass by the man with the ball and so become useless.

Both guards must keep their weight down low, close to the ground, so that the wedge, if directed at either, cannot throw that one at once off his balance backward. If this occurs, the wedge will always make its distance, perhaps go many yards. Lying down before the wedge is a practice based upon this principle of keeping close to the ground, and is by no means an ineffectual way of stopping an advance, although it is not as strong a play as bringing about the same result without actually losing the power to straighten up if the wedge turns. Moreover, the men in the front of a wedge are becoming so accustomed to meeting this flat defense that they not infrequently succeed in getting over the prostrate man and regaining the headway on the other side. This, as one can readily see, must always yield a very considerable gain.

When a run is attempted at some other point in the line, it is the duty of the guards to get through hard and follow the runner into his opening, even if they cannot reach him before he comes into the line.

In this class of play a guard should remember that if he can lay a hand upon the runner before he reaches the line he can spoil the advance to a certainty, for no runner can drag a heavy guard up into and through an opening. It is like dragging a heavy and unwieldy anchor.

A guard can afford to, and must sometimes, tackle high. Not that he should, in the open, ever go at the shoulders, but in close quarters he often has no time to get down low, and must make the best of taking his man anywhere that the opportunity offers. He must always, however, throw him towards the opponent's goal.

Another point for guards to bear in mind is, that in close quarters it is often possible to deprive the runner of the ball before he says "down." A guard who always tries this will be surprised at the number of times he will find the referee giving him the ball. He will also be astonished at the way this attempt results in the runner saying "down" as soon as he finds someone tugging at the ball.

A man gives up all thought of further advance the instant he finds the ball slipping at all in his grasp; and when his attention is distracted from the idea of running, as it is when he is fearful of losing the ball, he can never make use of his opportunities to good advantage.

For this reason the coach should impress upon all the forwards the necessity of always trying to take away the ball; but the men in and near the center are likely to have the best opportunity for this play, because it is there that the runner encounters a number of men at once rather than a single individual.

CAMP & DELAND:

A Block to Masses. When he meets the interference he should never be lifted up by the push, but must settle down, and, if he finds it crowding him back, go quite down on to the ground before it, and bring it to a standstill.

He cannot, in the close quarters of the centre, always tackle low, but he should always bend back anything he gets hold of, and should be no gentle weight when he hangs himself upon the man with the ball.

NEW YORK——THE GREAT FOOTBALL MATCH BETWEEN YALE AND PRINCETON, PLAYED ON THANKSGIVING DAY AT MANHATTAN FIELD.

THE TACKLES

WALTER CAMP:

Those teams upon which the work of end and tackle has been best developed have, for the last few years, been markedly superior in the opposition offered to plays of their opponents. This fact in itself is an excellent guide to the style of play one ought to expect from these two positions. The four men occupying them are the ones to meet nine tenths of the aggressive work of the opponents. The position of tackle, a position much later to reach the full stage of development than the end, has nevertheless now attained almost an equal prominence.

The tackle is an assistant to both end and guard, while he has also duties of his own demanding constant attention. As regards the relations between the tackle and guard, they are best defined by saying that the guard expects to receive the assistance of the tackle in all cases requiring agility, while in cases requiring weight the guard is equally ready to lend assistance to the tackle.

STAGG & WILLIAMS:

The tackle occupies the most important position on the rush line. It is possible to get along with a lumbering center and slow guards if they are able to block well and make good openings, but it is not possible to have slow tackles and play good football at the same time.

The tackle must be endowed with more than the ordinary amount of shrewdness and judgment. To a certain extent this can be acquired by long practice, but the tackle must be of quick perception and good judgment naturally in order to play the position in the best manner. Quickness in getting through the line, agility in avoiding interference, sure tackling, getting down the field on a kick, and running with the ball are essential qualifications to look for in selecting a man to fill the position of tackle.

CAMP & DELAND:

The Tackle. *Strength and Dash. Saves the End and Rush-Line Back.* After all this work by the end there is still left a little something for his more moderate-moving comrade — the "tackle" — to do.

He, the tackle, has the pounds and the strength, and must take good care of his end and his rush-line back. He will not let them pound themselves to pieces against the heavy packed oncoming mass.

He knows that they are both good men, and will not hesitate a moment, when it becomes necessary, to smash anything that comes, and for that very reason he appreciates the unsoundness of any play by him that shall leave heavy mass-meeting for these lighter and more high-strung bundles of nerves that flank him and pick the runner with an almost unerring certainty.

He, the tackle, therefore, throws himself in on the instant of the snap-back, and if he does not hit the runner he strikes the interference hard, and smashes as much of it back on the runner as he can; he stays with it as long as he can, and when he goes down and it goes over him he grabs what seems to be the tail end of it, and which usually is the man with the ball.

But if he gets nothing, he knows from his feelings that he has opened up a hole in it, and that one of his two tried friends is probably through that hole and anchored on the runner.

OFFENSIVE TACKLE

WALTER CAMP:

When his own side has the ball, the tackle has far more than the end to do. In fact, the tackle has the most responsible work of any man along the line, having more openings to make, and at the same time the blocking he has to perform is more difficult. The earlier description of the work of a line half and the tackle in getting through is sufficient to indicate the difficulties which the opposing tackle must face in preventing this break through.

While blocking may not be the most important duty, it is certainly the one which will bear the most cultivation in the tackles of the present day, for the ones who are really adept in it are marked exceptions to the general run. It is no exaggeration to say that more than two thirds of the breaking through that does real damage comes between the end and guard, and therefore in the space supposed to be under the care of the tackle.

By successful blocking is meant, not unfair holding, which sooner or later will result in disaster, nor backing upon a runner or kicker as the charger advances, which is almost as bad as no blocking, but that clever and properly timed body-checking of the opponent which delays him just long enough to render his effort to reach his man futile every time.

This kind of blocking looks so easy, and is so difficult, that it is found only in a man who is willing to make a study of it. Coaching can but give any one wishing to acquire this a few points; the real accomplishment depends upon the man's unflagging perseverance and study.

The first thing to be noted is, that a really good forward cannot possibly be blocked every time in the same way. He soon becomes used to the method, and is able to avoid the attempt. Dashing violently against him just as he is starting may work once or twice, and then he will make a false start to draw this charge, and easily go by the man.

Standing motionless, and then turning with a sharp swing back against him, will disconcert his charge once in a while. Shouldering him in the side as he passes will throw him off balance or against some other man, if well performed, occasionally. Falling down before him by a plunge will upset him even when he has quite a clear space apparently, but it will not work if played too often.

By a preconcerted plan he may be coaxed through upon a pretended snap, and then the ball played while he is guarded and five yards gained by his off-side play, but he will not be taken in again by the same method. These are but a few of the strategies which engage the study of the tackle.

In blocking for a run the case is very different, and depends upon the point of assault. If the run is to be made around the right end, for instance, by the left half-back, the right tackle must block very slowly and long. That is, he must not dash up to his man the instant the ball is snapped and butt him aside, for the runner will not be near enough to derive any advantage from this, and the opponent will easily recover in time to tackle him.

Rather should he avoid contact with his man until his runner makes headway, and then keep between the opponent and runner until the latter puts on steam to circle, when it is his duty to engage his man sharply, and thus let the runner pass.

In blocking for an inside run upon his own side, he should turn his man out or in, as the case may be, just as the runner reaches the opening, being particularly careful not to make the break too early, lest the opponent reach the runner before he comes to the opening.

STAGG & WILLIAMS:

On the offense, the tackle cannot leave any unprotected space between himself and the guard, if it be occupied by an opponent. He must therefore always take the inside man. This may require him to play close to the guard. From this position he must do all his running with the ball, all his blocking, all his interference for the runners, and make all his openings; varying his attitude toward his opponent to meet the special need of the moment.

In making his opening the tackle has to outwit and combat a very free opponent, one who, as a rule, is constantly changing his position. This renders it difficult, sometimes, to make an opening because frequently it has to be done while the opponent is changing his position, and when, perhaps, the tackle himself is not in a favorable position for making that particular opening. Likewise, when trying to block his opponent, the tackle must follow him closely and keep in front of him, and must be all on tiptoe to dart forward to get in a body check before the opponent acts.

CAMP & DELAND:

Play on the Offensive. On the offense he blocks, and blocks hard. When the run is coming his way he blocks long; when it is going on the other side, he comes away quickly and follows close. He may make runs himself. In that case he plans various methods of getting away free and cleanly from his vis-à-vis; he hugs the ball tightly as he takes it from the quarter, and, keeping his head down low to escape observation, he plunges into the line, never stopping as long as he can make his feet go.

Special Instructions for Blocking by a Tackle. Blocking by the tackle is but little less in importance than blocking by the guard. In certain plays the guard's position makes his blocking of greater relative value, but there are many operations in which the tackle bears a heavy load of responsibility for his blocking.

First of all, let it be understood that if the space between himself and his adjoining guard is occupied by any opponent, it is the tackle's duty to leave his own tackle and block this opponent instead. To use the language of the coaches, he must always "take the inside man." Thus, as a rule, the tackle will find that his blocking must be done in close proximity to the guard.

The position of the body differs somewhat from that assumed by the guard, for the tackle is a man whose activity must be much greater, and it will be better for him to take such a position as will make it possible for him to follow his opponent's every movement with lightning quickness. It will be better for the tackle to keep one foot slightly in advance of the other, letting the toe of the rear foot be about on a line with the heel of the forward foot. Keep well up on the toes, and avoid any tendency toward inertia. The tackle, in blocking, should be in almost continual motion. Follow the opponent closely, keeping well in front of him, and always on tiptoe, ready to start forward the instant the opponent attempts to go through. Expose no part of the body as a handle which the opponent may grasp. Keep the head high enough to prevent his seizing it; keep the arms close to the body, to prevent him from seizing them; keep the chest in a position where it is not exposed to a blow.

Finally, keep yourself squarely in front of the man opposed to you, and as close to him as possible. Watch him sharply; listen for the signal, and try and get away with it; remember that agility is the first requisite, and never allow your body to rest upon your heels or flat foot when you are in action.

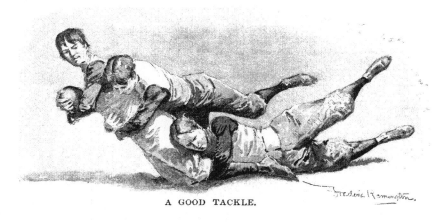

A GOOD TACKLE.

DEFENSIVE TACKLE

STAGG & WILLIAMS:

The name of the position indicates the work of the player. He is to tackle. The position which the tackle occupies in the line explains this, and it is best appreciated when it is understood that the tackles should take part in more than half the defensive work of the team.

The tackle occupies the most responsible position because he assists in checking two distinctly different styles of play. On the side toward the center he is to help the guard in blocking the heavy plunges which are frequently aimed at that point of the line, while on the other side he has to work with the end-rusher against all plays between them and on all plays around the end.

To play this position properly on the defensive, therefore, requires a master mind and an equipment of physical capacity and skill unequaled by any position on the eleven. The points mentioned are sufficient to show that the tackle should be a man of considerable weight, because he has to bear a great deal of the heavy plunging into the line. The greater the weight the better, provided, of course, that the other requirements are met.

As a rule, it is rare that a man weighing over one hundred and eighty pounds can meet these requirements, and it is more often that men weighing one hundred and sixty-five or seventy pounds are selected for this position on the best teams. The general build of the man also qualifies his usefulness.

The one hundred and sixty-five pounds will be much more effective in a man from five feet six to five feet ten inches in height than in one above that height. In truth, the man of stocky build can usually fill this position much better, because his weight is nearer the ground and he is always in a position to make a low tackle.

HOLDING THE RUSH LINE.

As a great deal of his tackling should be dashing and brilliant, right in the midst of interference where he must throw himself instantly, a tall man would be at a disadvantage. A thick-set, round-bodied man with large arms and legs would also be a much harder man to stop when running with the ball.

Of equal importance with weight, the points which should determine the selection of the tackle are agility, speed, and the ability to tackle in the face of interference. Even speed can to a small degree be dispensed with if the man is quick and agile and is a sure tackler.

The tackle must go through the line on the defense. The plan of waiting until it is seen where the run will be made and then running behind his line to help, if the play appears to be on the other side, is disastrous to a good defensive game. It not only is dangerous, because it leaves the way clear for a splendid run on a double pass, but it is also especially harmful because it gets the tackle into the habit of waiting for every play to become well started, and this is fatal to a strong defense.

When acting on the defensive the distance which he should stand from the guard and the manner of going through the line, either to the inside or outside of his opponent, should be determined by previous judgment as to where the play is to be made and influenced by an instantaneous perception as the play starts.

The position, too, must be taken with the utmost caution and selected at just the right distance from the guard to best meet the play and still be able to defend his position on either side. There is need of the closest and quickest observation and cleverest judgment. Moreover, as many of the plays cannot be determined beforehand, such a position must be taken as will best enable the tackle to check any play which can be made.

He must then be on the alert for the very first indications of the play and act on them, and at the same time he must still keep the closest watch for later developments which change the direction in which the ball will finally be carried. Playing up close to the guard is always dangerous unless it is necessary to do so in order to stop a wedge play, for the tackle could then be blocked in very easily from helping, if an attack were made on the space between himself and the end man, or in a play around the end.

He therefore would cut himself off from defending two-thirds of his territory and the most defenseless part of the line. Playing far away from the guard is also dangerous, for he then leaves the part of his territory which is nearest the opposing half-backs too much exposed and gives his opponent a chance to block him off from defending it.

Of course, if the tackle were free from the checking of an opponent, he could play some distance away from the guard and still defend the space between them; but the fact that there is a player opposite who is giving all his attention, wit, and energy to securing an advantage over him, gives a turn to the problem which he cannot ignore in making his calculations.

The tackle takes a certain position; the opponent takes one also. It may be a little to the right or a little to the left of him, or it may be directly in front of him.

The tackle may change his position a little and then the opponent perhaps change his, but their relative positions may, or may not, be changed; or possibly his opponent may remain in the same place.

Just this action or inaction on the part of the opposing tackle is sufficient to help him determine how he should play in his defense, and is one of the signs to be considered in deciding upon his own position and action.

The tackle should usually play right up to the line, on the defense. Sometimes with a very quick opponent, it may be better to play a little back from the line.

He should be restless, and on the alert for an opportunity to go through on the side of his opponent offering the best advantage. He should watch the ball closely and spring the instant it is snapped.

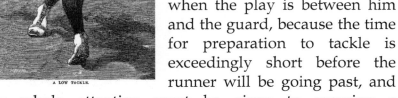

A LOW TACKLE.

His course of action in reference to his opponent must be to get him out of the way as quickly as possible. It may often be best for the tackle simply to drive his opponent back with hard, quick pushes.

This might frequently be best when the play is between him and the guard, because the time for preparation to tackle is exceedingly short before the runner will be going past, and the whole attention must be given to securing a momentary freedom from interference, for a quick spring.

The tackle has a great deal of this quick tackling to do because the runs are so frequently made in his region. Much of this also must be done right in the midst of interference, when the only chance to get the runner is by hurling himself headlong at him as he passes.

There are a variety of tactics which can be employed in getting through the line, and every tackle should be able to use them at will. Those are best which enable the tackle to get through quickly and at the same time permit him to watch the runner closely.

This is a point which ought to be deeply impressed on the minds of all the rushers. The situation changes so quickly when a run is being made that it is not safe to have the eyes off the runner for a second.

The methods usually employed in breaking through the line are: striking the opponent in the chest quickly and hard, and following it up with a shove to one side when he is off his balance; whirling suddenly around him, using either foot as a pivot; ducking quickly to one side; making a feint to go one side and going the other; striking the opponent with the head or shoulder and lifting him aside; stepping a little to one side as the opponent comes forward and swinging him through behind him.

DECEMBER 7, 1889.

A "TACKLE."

The tackle can sometimes secure an advantage for breaking through by pushing his opponent back from the line just before the ball is snapped. He must be very free to move, and go through with a jump. It is better to keep as low down as possible in doing this.

On end plays the tackle must break away from his opponent as quickly as possible. He will have no time then to carry his man before him except, perhaps for an instant, as he pushes him back to get by him.

Yet he must make sure to knock his opponent sufficiently off his balance to prevent his following him and giving him a shove at a critical moment.

In defense on an end play, everything depends on the tackle reaching the runner before he begins to turn in order to circle the end, and before he has swung in closely behind his interference.

The runner then has not yet gotten under full speed and the interferers are somewhat scattered and looking toward the end. The tackle has the best chance for defeating end runs; in this he is ably seconded by the end man, the two working together, in fine team play.

If the play is around the other end, the tackle should follow the runner around and try to overtake him. It is sometimes possible for a fast runner to do this when he breaks through quickly.

In following the man with the ball, the tackle must be on the watch constantly for a double pass. If he suspects one is to be made, he must be sure not to be drawn in or blocked as he runs behind the line. It would be better, in that case, to go straight through.

The tackle can do more to defeat a double pass than any other player, for, if he plays his position well, he will meet the runner when there is not more than one interferer to combat. If he then does not tackle the runner, he can force him to run so far back of the line that the rest of the team will be able to come to his assistance before he circles the end. The position which the tackle should take on the defense against mass plays from the center of the field is shown in the diagrams further on.

He should move off from the guard sufficiently to protect the side of the field and at the same time be able to spring back close to him on any play directly forward. It is his special duty to tackle the runner if he comes out at the side of the formation.

In case the runner does not come out before the opposing rushers meet, the tackle should dive in and secure him, if possible, but in doing this he must be careful not to leave too great a space between himself and the guard, as an opening through which to send the runner may be intended at that very point.

It is impossible to lay down rules of action for the tackle on wedge plays in the line. He must work according to his best judgment based on the situation; but an important factor in successful play will be to put in the work low down. If he is caught by the wedge in an upright, or nearly upright position, he will be rendered absolutely useless.

For this reason, it is often best to dive in at the side of the wedge about knee high and try to tackle the runner, or cause him to fall over him. If the wedge is revolving, it is often best for the tackle to fall down in front of it.

The tackle must consider it his first duty to assist the center and guards in checking the wedge, and leave the other players to attend to the runner if he comes out from behind or at the side.

A LOW RUNNER.

WALTER CAMP:

When the opponents have the ball and are about to kick, the tackle is one of the most active components of the line. He may not be moving until the ball is snapped, but upon the instant that it is played he is at work. He may himself go through to prevent the pass or kick, or still oftener he may make a chance for a line half-back to do this.

By a line half-back is meant that one who, upon his opponents' plays, comes into the line and performs the duties of a rusher. This method has become so common of late that it is well understood.

The play of this line half-back must dovetail into the work of the tackle so well as to make their system one of thoroughly mutual understanding. For this reason they should do plenty of talking and planning together off the field, and carry their plans into execution in daily practice until they become in company a veritable terror to opponents, particularly to kicking halves.

One of the very simple, yet clever and successful, combinations worked in this way has been for the line half to take his position outside the tackle, who immediately begins to edge out towards the end. This opens a gap between the opposing tackle and guard, for the tackle will naturally follow his man. This line half simply watches the center, and as he sees the ball played goes sharply behind the tackle and through the opening.

This play can be greatly aided by cleverness on the part of the tackle, who, to perform it to perfection, should edge out most cautiously, and with an evident intention of going to the outside of his man.

He should also watch the center play, and, most important of all, jump directly forward into his man when the ball is snapped. This will enable the half to take almost a direct line for the half, and with his flying start have more than a fair chance of spoiling the kick.

The tackle must not be idle after his plunge, but should follow in sharply, because there will always be an opposing half protecting the kicker; and if the line half be checked by this man, as is not unlikely, the following tackle has an excellent opportunity by getting in rapidly. The tackle and half should alternate in their arrangement, neither one always going through first, and thus add to the anxiety and discomfort of the opponents.

When the opponents are about to run instead of kick, the same combination of line half and tackle can be put in operation, except that it will not do for these two to follow each other through with such freedom, as there is too much danger of both being shunted off by a clever turn coupled with well-timed interference. The cardinal point to be remembered is, to be far enough apart so that a single dodge and one interference cannot possibly throw off both men. The tackle's duties towards the end have been partially described in dwelling upon the work of the latter, but there is plenty of detail to be studied.

One of the first things to impress upon the tackle is, that he must watch the ball, not only upon the pass from the quarter, but also after it settles in the runner's arms, for the most successful double or combination passes are those which draw the tackle in towards the center and give the second recipient of the ball only the end to pass.

It has been too common a mistake of coaches to caution a tackle who has been deceived by this double pass against "going so hard." This is wrong. It soon results in making a slow man of the player, for he hangs back to see if the runner be not about to pass the ball, until he is too late to try for the man before he reaches the rush line; and, with the present system of interference and crowding a runner after he reaches the rush line, there is no chance to stop him short of three, and it may very likely be five yards. The proper coaching is to send him through on the jump, with his eyes open for tricks.

Let him take a step or two towards the runner, so that, if no second pass be made, the tackle will be sure to meet him before he reaches the rush line, and not after it. This method of coaching makes not only sharp tackles, but quick and clever ones, with plenty of independence, which will be found a most excellent quality.

COLLIER'S WEEKLY   OCTOBER 20 1900

OUTSIDE THE TACKLE!

RUN OF A BACK WITH INTERFERENCE TOWARD AN OPENING MADE BY HIS MEN JUST OUTSIDE THE POSITION OCCUPIED BY THE OPPOSING TACKLE

THE ENDS

WALTER CAMP:

The end rusher must get into condition early. Unless he does, he cannot handle the work that must fall to his share, and the effect of a poor performance by the end is to produce disorder at once in the proportion of work as well as the quality of the work of the tackles and half-backs. This is not well understood by captains and coaches, but it is easy to see if one follows the play.

A tired end rusher, even one who has experience and a good idea of his place, will lope down the field under a kick, and by his lack of speed will allow a return; and, against a running game, while he will, it is true, force his man in, he will do it so slowly that the runner is enabled to pass the tackle. The first will surely result in his own halves shortening their kicks, and the second in drawing his own tackle too widely from the guard.

Both these results seriously affect the value of the practice for halves and tackles; consequently, the end must be put in condition early. The finer points of his position can be worked up gradually, but his endurance must be good at the outset, in order that the others may become accustomed to rely upon him for regular work.

But it sometimes happens that the captain or coach has no chance to make sure of this. His candidates may be raw, and only appear upon the first day of fall practice. In that case there is a method which he can adopt to advantage, and which answers the purpose. It is to play his candidates for that position one after the other in rotation, insisting upon hard playing even if it be for only five minutes at a time. In this way not only will the tackle receive the proper support, but the ends themselves will improve far more rapidly than under the usual method.

STAGG & WILLIAMS:

The end-rushers fill two of the most important positions on the eleven. The kind of man who could play a brilliant game at end, might not, perhaps, be able to fill any other position in the rush line, yet this is not necessarily true.

His qualification would be questionable only as regards build and weight. There are most brilliant end players who only weigh about one hundred and fifty pounds, and sometimes a little less, but the tendency now is toward selecting slightly heavier players for that position in order to gain more weight with which to meet the tremendous on-rush of the interferers. But it is not infrequent that the light, agile, cat-like men are much more likely to tackle the runner, and so are selected in preference to those possessing plenty of weight but less skill.

The tackling of these light, quick men is necessarily most brilliant, because they do not bore their way through to the runner but seize a momentary opening to put in their telling work.

Such a man, as has been said, could not play in any other position in the rush line, for he would not be heavy enough to stand the hard pushing and plunging to which, for example, the tackle is subjected. With the exception of meeting the end plays and plays between the end and tackle, the end-rusher does not have the hard, wearing work of the other rushers. Not that he does not have plenty of work to do, but he is not constantly combating an opponent and struggling with might and main to get through the line, thus being subjected to the little knocks and bruises which the other rushers have to endure.

CAMP & DELAND:

End Rush. *Experience and Physical Characteristics.* The position of end rush is one capable of the highest development of any along the line. For here a man can be at the same time a part of the rush-line and also a part of the half-back division. It requires cleverness in the highest degree, and experience is one of the most necessary qualifications, although it sometimes happens that a man with a natural instinct for the game will make such progress as to really entitle him to the position at the end of a single season. This is the rare exception, however, and usually the ends are men who have served a long apprenticeship in preparatory schools as well as on the second eleven. The end needs the greatest attention of the coach. Personally, a man for this position will probably be a lively, dashing player of wiry build, with no superfluous weight to carry, but muscular and quite capable of making every pound of that weight tell. For this very reason he must not be worked to death, and yet he must be kept up to the best performance always.

Condition a Prime Factor. For the good of the rest of the team in making their plays what they should be, the end must be put in condition early, and kept in good shape all the time. Hence, as noted in another chapter in this book, the coach must provide himself with a good supply of end material, and work the candidates alternately, so as to keep them all fast and active.

BLOCKING.

OFFENSIVE END

WALTER CAMP:

When his own side have possession of the ball, his play, like that of any other man, must be governed by the character of the intended move, and the knowledge of what this move will be is conveyed to him by the signal. The nearer the play is to his end, the greater is the assistance he can render. There is little need of coaching him to do his work when the run is along his line, nor, in fact, when it is upon his side of the center. The knowledge of the proximity of the runner stirs him up sufficiently, if he have any football blood in him. The point towards which coaching should be directed and where it is needed is in starting instantly to render assistance when the play is upon the other side of the line. There is no limit to the amount of work an end may perform in this direction.

A good end can toss his man back so that he cannot interfere with the play, and then cross over so quickly as to perform effective interference even upon end runs. In "bucking the center" he can come from behind with valuable weight and pressure. A coach should remember, though, that it will not do to start an end into doing too much unless he is able to stand the work, for an end had better do the work well upon his own side than be only half way useful upon both ends. A tired-out end makes the opponents doubly strong.

STAGG & WILLIAMS:

The end-rusher is at liberty to take any position he chooses on the offense. His one thought, however, should be to take that position from which he can best operate in helping out the play. Many end-rushers fail to do this.

Some ends play up in the line and follow their opponents wherever they move, no matter how far out they go. Others take a stand a little back of the line, about a yard or two from the tackle, shifting this now and then as the play suggests and admits. This latter is generally the best position which can be taken for helping in the interference, and it is also a better position from which to start if the end-rusher is to run with the ball himself.

Whenever the end-rusher is going to take the ball he should carelessly assume a position a little nearer the quarter-back–perhaps almost behind the tackle. Otherwise, the distance which he would be obliged to run before he reached his opening would be so great that the opponents would have enough time in which to intercept the play. On this play the quarter-back should give the ball to him by a short pass and then run ahead to interfere.

If the end-rusher plays up in the line he should always take the inside man when acting on the offensive. This is a point frequently forgotten, and oftentimes is the reason why end runs are stopped before the runner reaches the end. The end-rusher should also remember to help the tackle whenever the latter takes the ball. In this case, it may be necessary for the end-rusher to step in and block the opposing tackle, but if the tackle can break away from his opponent without assistance it is better that the end should follow the tackle right around. When the tackle is to go into the line the end can do no better than place his hands on his hips and steer him into the opening.

If the end-rusher does this well he can be of great assistance to the tackle in running, and at the same time prevent him from being caught from the rear. The best way to play the end position in making the different evolutions is shown in the chapter containing diagrams.

CAMP & DELAND:

On the Offensive. The duties of an end on offense are equally arduous. With the rapid advance in the science of the game in the last few years, he has become both a line man and a running half-back, — in fact, a good end may be used, on a pinch, as a half-back, either from his regular place at end, or he can actually substitute if there be a shortage in halves. As a runner from his own position he receives better interference than does the half or full back. Then, on the other hand, when the far half on his opposite end runs, he makes a most important part of the early interference by boxing the tackle or rush-line half.

A Few Words to the End Rush. Nothing need be added to the instructions already given, as the bulk of the blocking in the line is done by the three men playing respectively at centre, guard, and tackle. With the advance of the modern game the end rush is called upon to do almost no blocking whatever. In fact, he rarely plays in the line opposite to his opponent, and the blocking he is occasionally called upon to do is to assist the tackle to pocket his opponent. This blocking is of a different class from that which we have been considering. It is rather more in the nature of running blocking, and corresponds to "riding off" in the game of polo. From his position in the line, the end plunges forward, meeting the opposing tackle with his shoulder, striking him as low as the hip, and endeavoring to reach him before he has come clear of his immediate engagement with his own opponent.

HARPER'S WEEKLY. NOVEMBER 29, 1890.

FOOT-BALL—A COLLISION AT THE ROPES.—Drawn by Frederic Remington.

DEFENSIVE END

WALTER CAMP:

When the opponents have the ball, the end rusher must, in the case of a kick, do his utmost to prevent his vis-à-vis from getting down the field early under the ball. That is the cardinal point, and it is not necessary for him to do much thinking regarding anything else when he is facing a kicking game.

When his opponents are about to make a run, the situation is much more involved. He must then consider himself as the sole guardian of that space of ground extending from his tackle to the edge of the field, and he must begin at the touch line and work in.

That is, he must remember that, while on one side of him there is the tackle, who will do his utmost to help him out, there is on the other side–that is, towards touch–no one to assist him, and a run around the end means a free run for many yards.

"Force the man in" is always a good motto for an end, and one he will do well to follow conscientiously. To force the man in does not mean, however, to stand with one foot on the touch line, and then reach in as far as possible and watch the man go by, as nine out of every ten ends have been doing for two years. It means, go at the runner with the determination of getting him any way, but taking him always from the outside.

An end cannot tackle as occasionally does a half-back or back, slowly and even waiting for his man, then meeting him low and strong. An end always has to face interference, and good interference will bowl over a waiting end with ease. An end must go up as far and fast as he dares to meet the runner, and when his moment comes–which must be a selected moment–he must shoot in at his man, reaching him, if possible, with his shoulder, and at the same time extending his arms as far around him as possible. Many times this reaching enables an end to grasp his man even though a clever interferer break the force of his tackle. And when his fingers touch the runner, he must grip with the tenacity of the bull-dog, and never let go.

It seems almost unnecessary to say that a high tackler has no chance whatever as an end rusher. He may play guard or center, but before a man ever essays the end he must have passed through all the rudimentary schooling in tackling, and be such an adept that to pass him without the assistance of the most clever interference is an impossibility.

An end should be a good follower; that is, if the runner make in towards the tackle, the end should run him down from behind when interference cuts off the tackle.

This is one of the best points for cultivation, because it effactually prevents any dodging by the runner. If he fail to take his opening cleanly, a following end is sure of him.

This is not a safe point, however, to teach until the player has fairly mastered the ordinary end-work; for the tendency is to leave his own position too soon, giving the runner an opportunity to turn out behind him, and thus elude the tackle without difficulty.

A few years ago there was quite a fashion for the man putting the ball in from touch to run with it along the edge of the field. For some unknown reason this play seems to have been abandoned, but it is likely at any time to be revived, and the end rusher should therefore be posted upon the modus operandi of it, as well as the best method of preventing its success. The most popular execution of this maneuver was the simplest; that is, the man merely touched the ball to the ground and plunged ahead as far as he could until brought to earth or thrown out into touch. This was accompanied by more or less helpful interferences upon the part of his own end and tackle. There were more intricate methods, however; and surely, with the amount of interference allowed in these days, it is odd that the side line has not been more fancied by those who have generalled the great games.

There was one team a few years ago whose captain used to deliberately place the ball just inside the line on the ground, as though only thoughtlessly leaving it there, and then spring in, crowding the end rusher three or four feet from the touch line, while a running half, who was well started, came tearing up the field, seized the ball, and usually made a long run before he was stopped by the astonished halves.

Many also were the combination passes in which the ball was handed to the end rusher, who, turning suddenly with his back to the foes, would pass to his quarter or running half.

Of these close double passes at the edge of the field the most effective were those wherein the runner darted by just inside the touch line, and the weakest the ones wherein the attempt was made to advance out into the field. For this reason there ought to be no particular necessity for coaching any but the end rusher and the tackle upon means to prevent advances of this nature.

To the players in the center of the line there is no apparent difference whether the ball be played from touch in any of these ways above mentioned, or through the more customary channel of the quarter-back.

To the end and tackle, however, the difference is marked, because the runner comes so much sooner and the play is so greatly condensed and focused, as it

A SCRAP ON THE ENDS.

were, directly upon them. This player, like the end, should, when the ball is played from a fair, be very loath to plunge forward until the play is located, because in the present stage of development of the game one can be quite sure that the opponents will not play the ball from touch unless they have some definite and usually deceptive line of action. Without such it is by far the better policy to walk out the fifteen paces and have it down.

The quarter-back also has work to do upon side-line plays, in assisting at the edge as much as possible.
But to return to the end. The instructions to the end are to handle the ball as much as possible while the opponent is endeavoring to get it in, and thus make the work of that individual as difficult as possible; and, secondly, to plant one foot close to the touch line and the other as far out into the field as is consistent with stability, and to maintain that position until the play is over.

He must neither try to go forward nor around, but, braced well forward, hold his ground. If he does this, no runner can pass within three feet of the touch line, and outside of that the tackle can take care of him.

NOW LADS HEADS WELL DOWN.

STAGG & WILLIAMS:

In defense, their especial duty is to prevent the long runs of the game. It is an unusual thing for a long run to be made through the center part of the line on account of the support given the rushers by the quarter-back and half-backs. Let a runner once get around the end with one or two interferers ahead of him, as is usually the case when such runs are made, and he is likely to go a long distance down the field and not infrequently make a touchdown. In defending his territory against these runs the end stands at the most remote part of the field for assistance to be rendered him.

He is at the extreme part of the rush line and has no one close to him to help him.

His nearest neighbor, the tackle, must be depended on for most of the assistance, and when he cannot render it, the end is put to the test of tackling a runner preceded by a group of interferers. In such an emergency a deep responsibility rests upon the end-rusher, because he is probably the last man left to prevent a long run and perhaps a touchdown, producing a sensation akin to that of the full-back when he alone stands between the runner and the goal.

Moreover, the end-rusher has to meet the runner under most trying circumstances. The runner and the interferers have gotten well under way; they have passed the most dangerous spot in the line and are coming on at great speed. The interference is now more focused and effective in arrangement than it has yet been. There are more interferers and they are more closely bunched.

At the same time, the end well knows that he is an especial mark on all sides. He realizes that a particular man is appointed to do his utmost to check his play and that if this man fails to do it, the work is to be attended to by other interferers who come immediately after.

Under these difficulties in tackling and maneuvering, it is not strange that every captain is most careful in the selection and training of his end men.

CAMP & DELAND:

His Defensive Play. On the defense, outside of his relation to the tackle, the end has to be prepared always for short kicks, and for quarter-back or "on-side" kicks.

He should be ever ready to warn his line if he sees from his position of greater vantage any unusual formations being made, or any unaccountable preliminary move on the part of the enemy. He must also be ready to come back and assist his full-back when that player is handling a kick, and he must be quick to see and form an interference should his catcher have the opportunity for a run.

The really clever end may often be made the director of this play, and may call out to the catcher the instructions as to running or heeling the ball, although this is preferably the work of the backs. The end is also the man to be ready for a bad pass by the opponents, that goes past the intended recipient toward the edge of the field.

A fumbled pass is usually too far in toward the centre for the end to venture, and the tackle should lunge after that kind of a pass; but high passes, or passes too far in front of the runner, will come the end's way, and quickness to seize upon such an opportunity may mean a touch-down and perhaps a game.

Meeting Interference. As to the end's duties in meeting interference, one might almost fill up another chapter with this one phase of his play, for it is all important. But it is "a life that must be lived" to be appreciated. Calm, cold-blooded directions may help a man to learn to kick, or to run, or to block, but they seem almost tame when applied to that part of football known as breaking up interference.

The best description one can give of an ideal end in this respect is that he appears to be standing before an advancing wave of men as a swimmer about to plunge through the surf. As that wave strikes him he seems to cleave it apart, and, without apparent effort, appears standing behind the wave in the same expectant, waiting attitude as when it struck him.

Reaching the Runner. There are ends, and there have been ends, who apparently accomplished this, and, if one can get close enough to watch the eyes of such an end, he sees them fastened upon the man with the ball, and, whatever motion he may make with arms or shoulders in breaking the interference, he never takes his eyes off the runner, and hardly winks even as he is struck.

All this seems too strong to be true, and of course even the best end cannot always thus make way through and reach the runner. When the runner, for instance, is hugging his interferers very tightly, the end has to keep beating at the interferers with his hands and arms, pushing them, and backing away toward touch, leading the play out across the field, and slowing it up so that while he, by keeping comparatively clear of the mass, forbids the outlet of the runner, some one, say the far tackle, coming from behind, reaches the man with the ball; and no ground, or but very little, results from the play.

Again the mass may be moving too rapidly for such tactics, and yet too close to the runner to make it safe for the end to cut in. Then it may be necessary for him to go down against it, and bring it over him, taking a last chance on his knees of seizing the runner as the pile passes over him.

The layman, reading of such possibilities of end play, may be inclined to disbelieve in the willingness of a player to take such chances. It does look hard in cold type, but there are a dozen ends on every 'Varsity field ready to do far more dashing and plucky things than merely meet a formed interference.

NOVEMBER 3, 1881   HARPER'S WEEKLY.

A GAME OF FOOT-BALL—A "SCRUMMAGE" AT THE CLOSE.—Drawn by A. B. Frost.

FRANK LESLIE'S
ILLUSTRATED
NEWSPAPER

No. 1782.—Vol. LXIX.] NEW YORK—FOR THE WEEK ENDING NOVEMBER 9, 1889. [Price, 10 Cents. $4.00 Yearly]

A GAME OF FOOT-BALL—A STRUGGLE FOR THE BALL.
DRAWN BY J. DURKIN.

INTERCOLLEGIATE FOOT-BALL IN AMERICA.

This illustrates the typical feature of the American game in distinction from the English; namely, the open scrimmage. The ball is placed on the ground, and the snap-back stands with his foot or hand upon it, and when his quarter-back gives him the signal that all are ready he snaps it backward. The quarter receives it and passes it to another of his own side for a kick or run. The position of the players in this picture is excellent, showing, as it does, the points of play as one can see them only in an actual game. Beginning at the left of the picture we see the end-rusher of the side which has not the ball. With his eyes fixed upon the center with the keenest attention, he awaits the first movement of the ball to dash through at the man who is likely to receive it. His opponent stands watching him with equal intensity, ready to block him at the moment he starts. Next stands the tackle, apparently perfectly oblivious of the man facing him, and there is a confidence expressed in his attitude which assures one that this man, at least, will get through like a flash when the ball goes. Then there are two men, both stooping forward so that one sees but a leg of each. Of these two, one is the guard and the other the quarter-back, who, seeing a chance of getting through, has run up into this opening. The opposing guard is straightening himself up, in order to cover, if possible, both these opponents. If one may judge from appearances, however, he will be tumbled over most unceremoniously by the onslaught of the guard and quarter. The center-rush is braced for a charge, and with mouth open for breath awaits the first movement of his opponent. He, the snap-back, has just placed his foot upon the ball, and is ready to send it back as soon as the quarter, whose back and leg are just visible, shall give him the signal. The two men in the foreground are opposing guards, one of whom is ready to dash forward, and the other to block. The man who is about to block has his hands clasped, in order that he may be sure not to use them to hold his opponent, as that is an infringement of the rule. The other men in the rush line we can not see, but one can rest assured that they are as wide awake to their duties as the eager ones in view. Behind the group stands the referee with his arms folded and eyes intent upon the ball.

RELATIONSHIPS OF THE POSITIONS

CAMP & DELAND:

<u>DEFENSE</u>

Theory of Line Defense. If one could imagine that the arms of the players in the rush-line were as long as their possible tackling distance, the theory of the rush-line defense would be to have each man's finger-tips touch those of his neighbor, while the outer arms of the end rushers reached the touch line. Some teams of the past have been so nearly perfect in defensive play and tactics as to reach very close to this stage of the theoretical ideal. Beginning, then, at the outside, we say to the end and the tackle that the space from the farthest reach of the guard, out to the touch line, is in their care.

They have a rush-line half-back to aid them, and thus can count upon a certain greater freedom of action than in the old style of play, when the half-backs were kept more in the reserve. To limit the responsibility, it is fair to say that the end is solely responsible for the protection of the side line; that is, no matter what the excuse or provocation or temptation may be to draw in toward the field itself to help out the tackle, there is but one law for him that must not be broken, and that is "guard the edge."

Here again the addition of the rush-line back has made it possible, by the style of team play spoken of in the chapter on that branch, for the end to go in and help the tackle under certain circumstances.

Triangular Relation between the End, Tackle, and Rush-Line Back. The relation is almost a triangular one of tackle, rush-line back, and end, and any two of them may, at a pinch, "go in," but three never should go in. Suppose the play is directed exactly at the tackle. Some rush-line backs play on the line with the tackle. In that case the tackle or line-back goes through, according as one or the other has the better opportunity.

Whichever it is, he meets the interference, and endeavors to break it up, while his partner comes on behind, and takes the second turn at it, the end, meantime, covering the outside, but coming in as far as he can with safety, so that, if the interference actually engages the two, tackle and half-back, the end may take the runner as he comes free.

A Safe Stop for a Well-Protected End Run. Suppose, now, the run comes for the end. The inside man of the three is likely to be blocked or so tangled up in the interference that getting through in time to be in front of the runner is practicably impossible. Hence he can then be regarded as the safest man to help out the end by immediately going out, and as he goes out the end can come in, and with the tackle (or the second man, whether it be the tackle or half-back) smash the interference.

Having thus clearly defined the relationship of the end and the tackle in their defensive play, we make it possible for a coach to describe the duties and qualifications of both players with far greater directness than when merely handling each position by itself.

The Tackle's Inside Assistant. But the tackle has, like the end, some other good friends who are ever ready to back him up, so that he need never feel alone in his position. We have already spoken of the end and the rush-line back, and how, with the tackle, they make up a trio that on the defense should be a hard crowd to pass or put out of the way.

On the inside the tackle has still another helper, and one, too, of a different character. In the case of the end and half-back, the tackle has two indefatigably active workers, who can either of them move with greater agility than he; but, as we have already noted, the tackle knows that he must never rely upon these two for heavy work save in the direst extremity.

In the guard, however, he has a helper of quite another type. Here is a man not only the tackle's equal, but usually his superior, in the way of strength and weight, a big fellow who can plow into the heaviest mass like a bull, and who can always be relied upon to lift, and lift hard, when the attack is jammed up into the centre. For this reason the tackle always tries to turn the heavy plays in toward the centre where the guard and centre will be met, and where, if weight be required, it is always to be found.

Guard and Tackle on Fake Plays. In mentioning the tackle's intimate relation with his guard, we should say that this relation is not of such great importance as are the duties of the tackle toward the end, and his play with the rush-line back, save in mass plays and fake plays. In these two the guard-tackle play becomes vitally important. We will take up the fake plays first.

On the rush line

Suppose that the full-back pretends that he is about to kick, but the play is for the quarter to make a short pass to the half, who jumps straight ahead and tries to go through on his own side of the line. Although this play is frequently attempted outside the tackle, it is not a showy play, and seldom a successful one when sent outside. The trouble is that the necessary pause or length of pass is too great, and one of the three, tackle, rush-line back, or end, "nails" the man before he can get through.

The play — if it be properly worked as a "fake" — is far more likely to be a good one when directed inside the tackle. Here, then, comes the relation of guard to tackle.

The guard is big, and not as lively as end or tackle or rush-line back. But he can project himself with a plunge a long distance on account of his size, and it is his duty to do just this in the case alluded to. He throws himself sidewise at the breach which he is likely to see just as the man lunges forward at the opening. He usually barely reaches him, but comes near enough to get his hands or shoulder on the runner as he shoots through.

Relation of Centre Trio and Quarter. The relation of the centre trio and the quarter complicates the position of guard, for, in addition to the above-mentioned duty toward the tackles, the two guards, on defensive play, work with the centre and quarter. The principle, as will be seen in the chapter upon team play, is that of always getting some one man through on every play.

It is not always that the man is the quarter. The guard and centre may open up for him. But the two guards may also, on occasion, open up for the centre to go through, or the centre, quarter, and one guard make it so lively that there is an open space for the other guard to get through. All this can be planned and be in the hands of some one man of the four, who, as they are lining up, gives the signal indicating which method is to be used.

Still again, it is sometimes played by the centre trio "stretching" the opposing line out as far as they can. Here the tackles also assist, and the quarter may even come up into the line himself. This is not a safe method to be played too often, but is a very disconcerting one to the opponents when used judiciously.

This covers practically all the relations between the line men and their attendant backs on defense. In cases of kicks by the opponents, the relations are more properly a separation of one or more of these backs from the rush-line and the attendance upon the receiving full-back. The quarter may be the man to go back, or the half-back.

In either event the duties of the rush-line are, first, to attempt to spoil the kick or the pass, and then to assist either in interference for a run in, or, if the kick be returned, to get down the field. The ends get back as rapidly as possible to the aid of the catcher, interfering as much as possible with the opposing ends, and, in case of a run back, acting as the primary interferers.

OFFENSE

Relationships between the various positions in offensive play are so unlike those on defensive play that no general rules can be laid clown. We have noted a few, but each play forms a rule by itself, the first merit of many plays consisting in the fact that a different method is followed when the initial part of two or more plays may be exactly alike.

WELL BLOCKED.

OFFENSIVE LINE

CAMP & DELAND:

<u>BLOCKING</u>

When to Teach It. Blocking is the first principle in offensive playing. There can be no successful offensive work without good blocking. Hence it is the first rudiment which a line man must master, and too much attention cannot be given by the coach to this branch of rush-line work.

It is a well-established maxim that successful blocking must be taught in the first three weeks of the season. In order that there may be no mistake about the thoroughness of the instruction in blocking during this early period, it is well to require of the rush-line that they shall play at this time without interdependence or any relationship between man and man.

In other words, compel the team to win games from their earlier and weaker opponents of the season with the excellence of individual blocking only. Let there be no "theories of the defense" given to the line men until they are almost able to do without them; in other words, until they are able to meet strong opponents, and maintain their position by individual, unrelated efforts at blocking.

Two Divisions of the Subject. The rules for blocking may be divided into two parts: Instructions covering the general ground of blocking for any position in the line, and instructions which apply especially to the individual position and work of the player. We will take up the two divisions in their order, and give first, as briefly as possible, a few instructions for general blocking, under any circumstances and in any position.

Position in Blocking. As a rule, it is wise to get as close as possible to the man you wish to block. Take your position squarely in front of him, with legs and feet so placed that, while you can readily move in any direction, you are, nevertheless, so firmly planted upon your feet, and so squarely braced, that your opponent cannot push or pull you off your pins, or so far unsteady you that he can get free before you can recover.

As to the Feet and Legs. The position of the feet varies for different players; for the centre trio, the feet should be almost on a line latitudinally with the body; that is, neither foot should project to any appreciable extent ahead of the other.

For a tackle, however, one foot should be slightly behind the other, so that the toe of the rear foot will be about upon a line with the heel of the forward foot. This is about as wide an opening latitudinally as should ever exist between the two feet in successful blocking. A wider opening may give a better brace against a backward push, but it will make a man's movements much slower.

Before deciding just where your feet should be placed in blocking, make several tests and ascertain the exact position which you can best assume, and in which these two essentials may be provided for, — namely, that you can get away quickly; and that you cannot be knocked off your pins in any direction by the most savage onslaught of your opponent. A little experimenting will quickly determine the weak and strong points of any position you may assume. Above all, do not straddle, and stand on your toes, rather than on your heels or on the flat foot.

The heels should be used as secondary supports, against which you come back for a firmer brace, while your position on your toes will tend to extreme agility, and enable you to follow every movement of your opponent

without loss of time. Keep your feet under you in any case, so that you can be firm upon them; and then vary your position with every movement of your opponent. Keep the legs bent, and apply your power rightly. One pound of force rightly applied in blocking is better than five pounds applied at a disadvantage.

General Movement in Blocking. Keep as close to your opponent as possible. Watch every movement that he makes; wherever he goes you are to follow; especially watch his eyes as a cat would watch a mouse.

Do not look at his canvas, his belt, or, worse still, his feet. If his eyes cannot be readily seen in the position which you have taken look at his head. Keep your own head up. The ideal position for your body is to get low, well under your opponent, so that you can lift him up and run him back, if possible, the instant the play starts. Furthermore, by getting very low, you do not expose your chest to a straight blow. Keep the body high enough to prevent your opponent from seizing you by the head as he goes through, as this would speedily put you in a position where you would be of no possible help in checking the play. Concentrate your mind upon the problem of how to plunge into him at the moment that the ball starts. His eyes will probably be upon the ball; your eyes should be upon his eyes. The moment that you plunge into him, run him back out of the way, if possible, and make as large a hole as you can. If, by any mischance, your man should get by you, follow him, and run into him, or give him a running blocking-off before he can tackle.

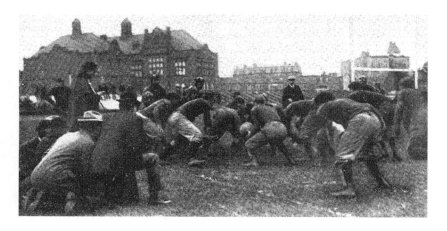

Comparison with Sparring. The best general idea of blocking may, perhaps, be gained by comparing it to sparring. In the latter sport your opponent is trying to hit you on some part of your body. In the present instance the same thing is true, if qualified by the fact that he is only doing this to aid himself in getting you out of his way; in order to parry his attack you must watch him, and if possible jump into him before he can plunge into you.

Go into him hard enough, if possible, to keep him out of the play, and then yourself instantly join the general interference. Strive always for the ideal position, which is to get your body directly across the path of your opponent in breaking through, so that your two bodies would form the shape of the letter X. Finally, listen closely for the signal, and let your blocking go with the play.

What is Body-Checking? Body-checking is a term which is generally synonymous with blocking, but in reality it is blocking in its highest development, for all blocking, properly, should be done with the body. The player should understand that the arms alone are never strong enough to block a man successfully; only to reenforce and supplement the action of the body, should the upper arms be employed.

A Common Fault with Young Players. A general error with inexperienced players is to try and reach too far with the body, and this weakens its resisting force. Wherever the body goes, the legs and arms should go with it. Keep the legs well bent under the body, until you are ready for the final movement of straightening up and putting all your force against your opponent as the ball starts in play.

You can scarcely go into your opponent too strongly at this last decisive moment. The old expression, often used by coaches, "pile into him like a ton of bricks," is not so far wrong after all.

Other General Hints on Blocking. When you are blocking an opponent close to the line, do not yield an inch. Be careful not to let him get a grip on your outside arm, for it would be of immense assistance to him in going through the line.

Remember that your brace must not be merely against a backward push, but equally against a forward pull, or a sideways plunge. In other words, it must stiffen you against a throw in any direction.

Always block your man away from the play. It is fair to assume that you can successfully check his onslaught for a brief interval of time; and your blocking should be so directed as to prevent him from reaching the runner at the point at which the runner will be after this first interval has elapsed.

In other words, if you are blocking a tackle for a run around the end, you would naturally block him on the outside, for it would be reasonable to assume that if you force him to go inside of you he would scarcely get clear from you until the runner had reached a point from which your opponent could not check him, except from behind.

Be careful in your blocking not to give away the direction of the play. This is a fatal error, into which, the inexperienced player will fall unless he watches himself.

Different Kinds of Blocking. Certain special occasions call for slight differences in the method of blocking, and it may be well to say here a word on three of these variations. We will classify them as "body-checking," "blocking hard," and "blocking long."

Body-checking. Body-checking implies temporarily checking the progress of an opponent, rather than  preventing his final movements.

It is well illustrated in the work of an end going down the field under a punt; while not lingering to block before he starts, he is, nevertheless, expected to slightly body-check an opponent in the rush-line, with a view to giving more complete protection to his own kicker.

Blocking Hard. Blocking hard is a term used to designate the kind of blocking which a man must do who is stationed on either side of the hole through which the runner is to pass.

When we tell a man to "block hard" it means that the exigencies of this particular play require of him a special effort or spurt. He is to play his strongest card; he is to sharpen every faculty and redouble every energy. The whole success of the impending movement depends upon him. His blocking for this one encounter must be absolutely sure. This is all summed up in the brief instruction, "Block hard."

Blocking Long. Blocking long is a term used to cover those exigencies which require that the resistance to the opponents' movements shall be maintained during a considerable interval of time.

When a player "blocks hard" he concentrates all his energy, and expends it in the briefest interval, during which he has his opponent completely at his mercy.

If, on the other hand, he "blocks long," he so husbands his resources and his strength that he keeps his opponent from interfering with the play for a period of time nearly twice as long as the usual period covered by ordinary blocking.

"Long blocking" is, perhaps, the most difficult of any for the average player to acquire. It is not easy to lay down special rules for his guidance. It is, rather, a faculty which will come to him intuitively, as he studies different opponents and learns more of the principles of primary blocking. He will find that there are certain methods by which he can block one opponent for a considerable interval of time, which will be wholly useless when he tries them upon another opponent.

Different men have different styles of play, which must be met by different tactics. In general, the position we have described, in which the bodies of the two men take the form of the letter X, is a sure position for long blocking.

A TOUCH-DOWN.

OPENING HOLES IN THE LINE

Interference and Shepherding. American Inter-collegiate football has a monopoly of the interference principle as applied to the breaking of a rush-line. In Australian football there is such a thing as assisting the runner, but this "shepherding," as it is called, is in no sense like our methods, and it is performed almost entirely in the open. In fact, in the Australian game, as soon as a mass of players get together the referee immediately blows his whistle, and the ball is put down.

Our interference is the product of the growth of many years. With our original adoption of the Rugby Union Laws we took over the principle of "on" and "off" side, and for several years lived fairly close to the traditions.

Heeling Out. The first step of variation from these traditions we took in the heeling out of the scrimmage. In this we are by no means alone, for the Canadians have also adopted heeling out, and it is the only natural outcome and relief from the monotony of the old tight scrimmage, with its stupid pushing. But with the heeling out was involved the question of the rights of the rush-line after the ball had been heeled back. Theoretically, every one of the side which had heeled back the ball was "off-side," for he was in a scrimmage, and had placed himself, or rather been placed, between the ball and his opponents' goal. There was no escape from the conclusion that he was infringing the rule.

But this was also true in almost any scrimmage, even if played in tighter fashion, for an absolute line drawn through the ball could hardly fail to cut off men here and there during the pushing. Besides, it was impossible in the tight scrimmage to be sure where the ball was at any moment, and frequently, as it popped out, the men were still pushing, so that, on the whole, it did not seem that the infringement would be much more heinous in the case of heeling out than in the older tight scrimmage.

The Development of the Use of the Arm by Forwards. The men in the line could not, of course, vanish into thin air the moment the ball was sent behind them, but at first they did the next most appropriate thing. They stood still where they were, or tried to run down the field in case they expected a kick. But it was not long before they found how serviceable an occasional extended arm was in cutting off an opponent who was going through to tackle the runner. From this it became the custom for the rushers to extend their arms as far as they could when lined up for the scrimmage, and thus give all the protection possible to their runner.

It was, however, traditionally improper to bend the arm at all in order to hold the opponent. Strange as it may seem, this tradition was lived up to for several seasons with a fair measure of propriety, but at last the temptation became too great, as the end to be secured seemed more important, and there came a year when our rush-lines reached out and held their opponents whenever the opportunity offered. This would naturally, unless corrected, have speedily put an end to the sport, for there could be no satisfactory tackling under such license.

Legislation against Holding. The players were themselves quick to see this, and at once began to consider legislation directed towards the abuse of holding. Two or three informal meetings between players of prominence at the universities finally led to a formal meeting and a very excited debate upon the matter. The result was, however, satisfactory. The convention took the bull by the horns, and enacted that the forwards of the side which had the ball should not use their hands or arms to block the opponents.

This was the first actual recognition of the distinction made between the side having the ball and the side trying to get through, and it was eminently proper that if we were to drift away from the strict "on" and "off" principles of Rugby Union, we should have some idea where we were eventually to arrive, and, until this distinction was made, the future of the sport looked problematical.

Saving the Game. The adoption of the five-yard advance rule had already saved the sport once from utter extinction when the block game threatened it so seriously, and now in another emergency the rule makers had found a satisfactory solution of a hard problem.

It was in this way that the making of holes in the line came to be a recognized part of American Intercollegiate football, and any one becoming a student of the game should bear in mind the origin of this part of the play, as it accounts for and reconciles many apparently arbitrary distinctions. The principle that the men between the ball and their opponents' goal have lost their right of way is the one that explains the underlying thought of the laws. But we do not hold, as was indicated and foreshadowed when we recognized interference, that the loss of the right of way means as much as the Englishman takes it to mean. He would view our interference as atrocious off-side play, and quite properly so under his rules. But we, after making it legitimate to obstruct an opponent so long as the hands and arms were not made use of in the act, have gone on developing our plays along that line until recent momentum and mass plays have made it necessary to call a halt.

MAKING AN OPENING FOR A RUNNER.

This brief history shows how we have arrived at "opening holes in the line," and also how far such breaking a path for the runner is recognized as legitimate.

The Hole should fit the Play. The cardinal point for the men making a hole in the line to bear in mind is, "What is the object of the hole?" A hole may be opened merely to deceptively draw the quarter and a half-back over to that side of the line. Such a hole should be opened early, and as widely and with as much demonstration of force as possible. The men who, like the quarter and half, are behind the line are seldom able to closely follow the course of the ball, and they depend more upon the appearance of the line to tell where the attack is being made than upon any ability to actually see the man with the ball. Here demonstrations like that mentioned above are often wonderfully effective in drawing these protecting and defensive players over to the wrong side of the line.

Then, too, a hole may be opened for the purpose of distracting the attention of the opponents from a  projected kick. Such a hole should have plenty of openers about it, and in this latter case it is also practicable to make it large and long, because the men engaged in making it are not needed later in any interference, as is sometimes the case in a criss-cross run or double pass.

Opening for a Plunge, and Opening for Long Interference. Coming now to legitimate openings, there are different varieties of openings necessary for different runs.

The opening for a plunge through the line on a fake kick, where the half dashes through on his own side of the line, should be not much more than merely keeping the opponents in their tracks and preventing their falling or throwing themselves down across the opening. It is a very small hole that is wanted, and that only for an instant of time.

Farthest removed from that style of opening is that required for a "round the end" run (that is, practically, between the end and tackle), with the swinging interference that such a run entails. This opening is usually effected by the end and tackle boxing in the tackle while a part of the interference forces the end out.

The opening must be a wide one, for anything less is likely to be choked up before the runner can get by.

Time of the Opening. It is this kind of an opening that requires long blocking, for the runner must follow his interference, and should not be forced to cut loose from it too early in the usually vain attempt to go through alone. How early such an opening should be made depends upon the starting speed of the runner and his interference, but it is safe to say that the later the real opening comes, so long as it comes before the main interferers reach the turn, the better; for it then enables the men to hem in the rush-line half, whereas, if the opening be made early, he will extricate himself in time to smash the interference before it gets well into the line.

What Happens when a Hole is Made at the Wrong Time. Interference met behind the line almost invariably loses half its dash through lack of confidence, and goes back against the runner, taking the pluck out of him as well. On the other hand, if the interferers once fairly reach the opening, they are confident as well as strong, and the feeling that they have already partly gained their end often enables them to carry the runner well past the difficult spot. The runner himself seldom gets on his real swing and dash until he actually feels that he has reached the striking point — then he has every muscle tense and he makes his supreme effort. For all these reasons, therefore, the opening should be rather a trifle late than too soon.

Opening for Tackle Run. An opening for a tackle coming around should be of a different character from that made for a running back. The inside man around whom he is to circle should crowd his opponent back as well as to the inside, while the man outside his opening may, if he be clever, even let his opponent through after a momentary blocking, provided he make him go on the outside and give him a little push onward with the shoulder as he goes by. The same is also true of the opening for a guard when performing a similar run.

Opening for Mass Play. Openings for mass plays striking the line at guard or centre are wholly different again from any thus mentioned. These openings are not made until the push part of the play has practically lost its force. As long as the mass is moving forward, it is utterly bad football to make any opening. Progress is all that is wanted, and the line men in front of the mass should stick together shoulder to shoulder until they find themselves brought almost to a standstill; then, with a final effort, they tear themselves apart, carrying a break into the opposing wall through which the runner, with the added push he is receiving from behind and from the sides, slips, and, should he come clear, steps out for himself

YALE VS. UNIVERSITY OF PENNSYLVANIA, NOV. 11, 1893.—THORNE (YALE LEFT HALF-BACK) GOING FOR "TACKLE AND END" HOLE BEHIND INTERFERENCE.

An opening made before the mass has done its work almost invariably means an alley way for the opponents to reach the runner and stop him before he has gained a foot, and sometimes with actual loss of ground.

Don't Open the Door for the Enemy to Come In. *Don't open the door for the enemy to come in, but for the sortie to go out.* And this leads us to another maxim that the line men should always bear in mind. In all mass or push plays the door must always open outwards. In runs by the tackle and guard, the door may open in, but the hinges must be on the outside. A door opens outward when the runner's men who line the opening are in opponents' territory; it opens inward when the opponents have broken through the line, but are pocketed or blocked off to either side. When a team has thoroughly possessed itself of the idea that there must be no double hinge in these doors, that under no circumstances must the door slam back into the faces of the bunch of runners, then that team has reached a time of high development — the time when its greatest game should be played.

To carry out the idea of the door in the line, let us take up an ordinary push play between guard and centre. Here imagine that the door is a double one, its two sides formed by the guard and centre. The play starts, the pushing mass crowding directly upon these two men, with the runner in a straight line behind the crack that will eventually become an opening between these two line men. Everything moves ahead a step or two, then, as progress becomes checked, the guard swings himself forward and out toward the tackle, the centre swings himself forward and out toward his other guard, and the mass of tightly packed players with the runner, and possibly the quarter at its peak, goes through the opening doors as they sweep aside the attacking party.

YALE VS. UNIVERSITY OF PENNSYLVANIA, NOV. 11, 1893.—BUTTERWORTH GOING THROUGH THE CENTRE WITHOUT INTERFERENCE.

How the Door Opens for a Tackle Run. Next, take the run by a tackle between the tackle and end. At the instant that the ball is put in play, the tackle on the side toward which the run is coming, manages to get squarely in front of his opponent. The chances are that that opponent does not desire to go inside, but has been instructed to go outside his man. This the tackle will have been able to discover with a fair measure of certainty some time earlier in the game. If he is sure of this he can take a decided step outward just as the ball is put in play, protecting the inside course slightly by keeping his leg and thigh still in front of his man.

At the same moment the half jumps boldly forward, and to the outside of the tackle. On some teams the end also closes in quickly. The far half and the full-back make straight for the space well out, but still inside the opposing end.

The door that is now opening may be imagined again as a double door, but it does not swing as in the push play. On the contrary, the outside half of it is opening in; that is, the man farthest from the runner reaches the line first, and the man just behind him is the inside man, and between them they should pin the end, who at the last moment sees that he must come in to reach the runner.

The inside half of the door, formed by the tackle, half, and end, is opening out, the end being the farthest toward the opponents' goal, the half next, and the tackle at the hinge. This half of the door should pin behind it the opposing tackle and rush-line half as the runner himself goes through, aiming in a diagonal line for the edge of the field, and only turning in after he passes his own end

YALE *VS.* UNIVERSITY OF PENNSYLVANIA, NOV. 11, 1899 – BUTTERWORTH (YALE FULL-BACK) SCORING THROUGH THE CENTRE.

We speak of this door opening in, with the hinge on the outside, because, as the tackle comes, the inner half of the door formed by the tackle, half, and end is much less movable and performs its duty satisfactorily if it merely holds its own, while the outer half, having only the end against it, appears to him as the real door, and toward that he runs, almost rubbing his shoulder along it as he goes through. It must open in, of necessity, since the end has probably so far advanced that he will be met inside the runner's territory.

Classification of Openings under this Head. Almost all openings may be classed under one or the other of these two heads. Straight runs into the line are after the fashion of push plays, except that the door opens sharply, and before the runner quite reaches it. "Around the end" runs are usually made inside the end, and the door is like that for the run of a tackle or guard.

Detail of Individual Work in Making Openings. As for the individual work in opening holes, there is a chance for a great variety of detail. A player may not use his hands or arms, but he can use his shoulders, his head, his neck, his hips, and his thighs, and it is only necessary for a skeptic to line up against a first-class guard or tackle to see how thoroughly an accomplished man can perform his work, and still make no use of hands or arms. Some men will fairly wind themselves about an opponent like a huge snake, while others will obtrude such a variety of obstacles in the shape of shoulders and knees as to make an insurmountable barrier at the proper moment.

The usual fault and the tendency to be combated in most line men is that of opening the holes too early and getting their weight too high at the outset. The player should try to straighten up as he opens the hole so as to prevent the opponent from reaching or lunging over him, and getting at the runner; to this end he should begin at a low point, and *stiffen up* rather than *settle down*.

After the Runner has Gone Through. As soon as the opening has let the runner through, those who have made it should abandon it, and push from behind forward into the mass, or follow the runner if he has gone through singly.

A RUN BEHIND INTERFERENCE.—Drawn by Frederic Remington.

INTERFERING FOR THE RUNNER

English and American Right of Way. In the chapter upon opening holes in the line we have already given something of the history of the growth of interference in the American game. In that section will be found an explanation of the "right of way," as observed in the American traditions. In English Rugby there is no such thing as interfering for the runner, and such an act would meet with the strongest disapproval of any one grounded in British beliefs as to off-side play.

Aid to the Runner. In order to appreciate the American methods one must begin with the premise now admitted in all our rulings, that it is perfectly proper, under certain restrictions, for a comrade to aid one of his side to get through the line, and to evade the attempts of the would-be tacklers. This assistance is usually rendered by the interposition of his body between the runner and his opponent or opponents. This assistance, as given by the line men in opening holes through which the runner may quickly pass, has already been dwelt upon at length. But it is not in the line that the art of interference reaches its perfection. It is rather in the long swinging runs out toward the end, or in the more closely formed mass plays hurled against a yielding spot in the opponents' front, that one sees interference in its highest development.

Theoretical Perfection. Its greatest possibilities can be best conceived when one realizes that, after the ball has been placed in the runner's hands, there are ten of his comrades who have no part to play save to assist him in making as long a run as possible; also, that there are but eleven opponents to stop him, one at least of whom (the full-back) is deterred by caution from entering into the attempt to catch the runner until that individual shall at least have come past the line of forwards, and started for the goal.

And so, in an ideally perfect interference, each man of the runner's side should take a man. This would leave only the full-back to stop the runner, and it is notorious that not the best tackler in the world can stop a thoroughly expert runner and dodger, save by overtaking him from behind. So, in a perfectly organized interference, touch-downs should be the ordinary results of possession of the ball.

Man-to-Man Interference *vs.* Line Interference. No such perfection has been reached, and yet, with the development of new and original plays, we are advancing toward the attainment of a degree of skill in this line that makes the study of defense indeed a hard one.

Before legislation was passed rendering it obligatory upon a side to actually kick the ball into the opponents' territory at kick-off, — thus practically surrendering possession of it, — it was by no means out of the range of possibility to steadily advance the ball by successive methods of interference from the middle of the field to a touch-down. At times this was accomplished by a succession of short advances, again by two or three long runs out toward the end. Many have been the plays based upon the supposition that the attainment of a man-to-man interference mentioned at the outset of this chapter was a practical possibility.

Probably there has never been a coach who has not been at times carried away with the belief that such an interference can be arranged. It is not for us to say that it cannot. But the evidence of the games of the past is against it. Occasional plays partaking of this method may be used, and used to advantage, but there is too large an element of chance about it to make it a good base plan for general development of successful interference.

DOWN!

There are better foundations to be laid in other theories, and the best of these theories is that one which depends upon the principle of dividing the opponents. This principle can best be illustrated by supposing that a line of men is running across the field in a diagonal direction between the opponents and the man with the ball. If these men could preserve just the right distance between each other, it is easy to see that it would be almost impossible for the opponent to reach the runner.

While there are many off-shoots of the theory of individual man-for-man interference, and while it is undeniably true that there are a number of minor plays that can and should be executed under an interference based upon this principle, the theory of line interference offers so much more possibility of practical field development that we set it down unquestionably as the one to be adopted as a basis for the general expansion of all plays.

Method of Line Interference. The first step in studying this method, in order to arrive at a thorough understanding of it and its application, is to consider the interference line as cutting off a certain section of the opponents' team from participation in the play.

This is wholly different from the man-to-man cutting off, and it is not directed at certain individuals *wherever they stand*, but at a certain section of the field, and it affects, therefore, the men who chance to be in that section.

If they stay out of that section, they will not be disturbed until the second movement of the play — the cutting off of another section of the field — commences.

Example of Line Interference. By way of illustration, let us take a simple run by a full-back through a space lying between the positions occupied by the opposing tackle and end. We arrange that a line of two or three men shall run diagonally, so that, just as the runner reaches the line, they may interpose between the path of that runner and the main body of the opponents. On the other side of him we may arrange for two or three other men to interpose between his pathway and the end rusher of the opposing line. That puts the case with the greatest degree of simplicity possible, and yet shows the entire theory of the first step in forming effective interference.

Second Step. The next step is after the same order. We have a runner moving between two converging lines of men. At a certain point this protection must cease because the runner and his interference must move with rapidity, or else the opponents, with their additional weight, will push through or crowd the interference against the runner. If both the interference and the runner are moving at high speed, the runner will eventually outstrip his interference. In fact, that is what he is expected to do in line interference. The passage through which he eventually emerges is called the outlet. If he goes clear to the end of the alley formed by his two lines of interferers, the play is simple, and, though effective, there is nothing in it to deceive the opponents, and the chances are that, though the runner will gain such distance as his interference is able to cut off for him, he will be met at the outlet, and there his run will come to an end.

Final Outcome. But now let us imagine the lines of interference considerably prolonged, and that when the runner has gone half way down the alley the interference is turned at almost a right angle, and the opening thus altered to another point. Such a move would deceive the opponents, and might add another chance of the runner's emerging at an unexpected point, and thus adding a long run. It is hardly practicable to actually turn the entire line of interference sharply, but it is possible to effect the same result by sending the runner through the side of it, and by making use of an extra man or men on the outside, practically forming a new interference as the old breaks up, and aiming that new interference in another direction.

Funnel-Shaped Alleys. In all this there must be borne in mind the advisability of having the alleys funnel-shaped, that is, in both primary and secondary interference, the end at which the runner is expected to enter the alley should be broad and well-opened, narrowing down from that to a small point at which he eventually emerges. This not only enables him to run straight for the most unprotected point of his opponents' line, but also makes it more difficult for more than one of his opponents to follow him from behind and thus prevent his escape if he be slowed up.

Combination of Primary and Secondary with Man-to-Man Interference. The most effective, but the most complicated in appearance of all interference, is that which, following out these two moves (that is, first a primary interference, which resolves itself into a secondary line), terminates in an outlet at which the runner is joined by a single interferer who has reached that point in time to precede him on down the field.

Of course, with this may be combined a man-to-man interference performed by the one or two who could not get into the primary or secondary interference, against the man or men most likely to reach the final outlet or to get in the later path of the runner after he emerges. The possible expansion of interference carried on along these lines is almost unlimited.

Walking Through the Interference. To come now to the detail of it. With a team of veterans fairly proficient in the general practice of interference, new plays may sometimes be added without going through the drudgery of slow and careful performance.

Unfortunately, however, for the work of the coach, there is seldom a team composed of all veterans, and so it is almost invariably necessary to walk through the plays and take up the interference gradually, accustoming each man to his position and his duty, and accommodating the speed little by little to the exigencies of the performers.

In walking through plays especial attention should be paid to the precise point at which the runner receives the ball, and the exact position of each player at that moment. It will be found that that is the moment of time about and by which to regulate the play.

Three Points of Measurement. There are three positions at which a measurement can be taken to define the relative places of the men who act as interferers with the runner. The first is when the ball is put in play; the second, when the runner receives it; and the third, when the runner makes his break, — that is, attempts to go through the outlet. At the first of these three periods of the play there are three points for consideration: the protection of the quarter during his pass, the deception of the opponents regarding the direction, and the quick starting of the entire body of men used in the play.

At the second period — when the runner receives the ball — there are two principal considerations: first, to render its reception secure, and with that is involved the question as to which side of the quarter or the half back certain interferers should pass; and, secondly, to protect the runner for a moment from behind in case a man shall have broken through too rapidly, and with this goes, naturally, protection in case of a poor pass or a fumble by the runner when attempting to take the ball.

At the third period — that is, when the runner makes his break on his own account — there are two great considerations to be observed: first, how to make his opening as safe from obstruction by either friend or enemy as possible; and, secondly, how to push or drag him along in case he fails to come free.

Addition of Double Passes. Having reached this stage in the analysis of the method of interference, we have placed in the coach's hands the material from which to build up all the necessary walls about his runner. Every play may be, and should be, studied by this process.

We now come to the still more complicated problem offered by the addition of double or even triple passes. By this term "double pass" we here mean either criss-cross or double pass, for it is general among players to distinguish these two by using the term "double pass" with the meaning that the ball be passed on in the same general direction; while by "criss-cross" is meant a pass whereby the ball is then carried by the second runner in the opposite direction, across the field.

We have already noted that it is not practicable to alter suddenly the direction of a moving mass of men, and that to alter the course of interference to good effect requires the addition of one or more interferers not involved in the

first line. But in the fact that the ball may be passed, and thus the position of the man with the ball be suddenly altered, we have an opportunity

of accomplishing almost an equivalent to a sudden change in the direction of interference.

And herein, as will be shown by some of the diagrams of plays in this book, we have possibilities thus far only partially appreciated and little understood. An ordinary double pass or a criss-cross is crude when compared with the same play elaborated by secondary interference, the primary being used not only to protect the first runner, but also to thoroughly involve the enemy at a point which suddenly becomes an unassailed point; while, at the same time, the whole force of perfected interference is sent at the spot which is left comparatively unprotected. Add to this the simplicity of using the same play with a variety of outlets, so that the very energy of the opponents will prove their own undoing, and one can gather something of the importance of these new movements.

Final Perfection of Interference, with Double Pass and Kick. Still beyond this may be placed the hitherto utterly neglected feature of play involved in altering by a kick all the momentarily existing conditions, and we come to a stage of perfected assault (consisting of a combination of primary and secondary interference rendered still more menacing by a double pass, and with a finally altered situation due to the placing of the ball by means of a kick far in advance of the actual runner) that may well give those on the other side, in whose charge lies the problem of defense, some bad hours of consideration.

When a runner breaks with, let us say, but three men to pass, and deliberately punts the ball over the head of the full-back, after approaching as near as he can with safety, he and his companions who are going down the field prepared for this final manoeuvre will, in many cases, have a far better chance than the opponents of regaining possession of the ball, and with that possession the coveted touch-down.

This chapter, however, is not intended to deal with specific plays, but rather to lead up to the development of such theories of interference as shall make captains and coaches able to plan out, not a few plays that are already public property, but absolutely new plays which emanate from their own study, and which depend for success merely upon their perfected execution.

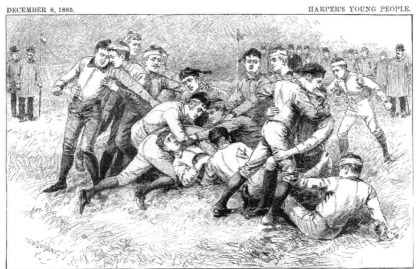

A COLLEGE FOOT-BALL MATCH—A SCRIMMAGE.

THE LINEMEN IN TEAM PLAY

Men in a Complete Interference. Such an interference, to be perfect, should carry a guard, quarter, and one back, with the runner, around the peak. One of these three goes over or out in making sure that the last man of the enemy's extended line dies without a chance of following.

The extra men who, beside the above, assist in the long interference may be the far end and the third back. Thus we shall have in a complete interference the quarter, guard, two backs, and an end. (This chapter will not deal with the plays themselves, but a reference to other chapters of the work will show the exact position of the individual players in the execution of various kinds of interference.)

How Line Men should Work. The next step in the general training for offensive team play is the blocking of the line men. Naturally, this is a part of the individual department as well, but it is so necessary to the development of team play that it requires a few words under this head.

Ordinary blocking consists of merely preventing the opponent from getting through and spoiling the play. Blocking in the team sense adds the feature of getting the opponent into the most unfortunate position possible, so far as his hopes of taking any part in the subsequent stopping of the runner is concerned.

For example, it is far better to get an opponent moving in the opposite direction from that he eventually finds he should have taken, than to merely hold him in his position, for in the first case he also interferes with his own men, who may have diagnosed the play better than himself. This is the underlying principle of team play in blocking — to make the opponent actually help in the interference.

Next, the forwards should be ever ready in case of emergency to take hold of their own runner and drag him forward. In almost all line plays there comes a moment when, before the runner has gone down, he is so situated with regard to one of his own rushers as to make it possible for that rusher to give him a pull of several feet, perhaps even yards. It has often happened, on account of this unexpected variety of assistance, that a runner is not only helped along, but even shaken free and put securely on his feet again for a run.

Aside from this added gain, it is the part of the forwards to always give their backs physical assistance in getting on their feet when the play has to be particularly continuous in point of repeated plunges by these three men.

With this help, and the moral force of such encouragement, three good backs can smash a stout line for fifteen minutes at a stretch, before they lose their dash.

DEFENSIVE LINE

CAMP & DELAND:

BREAKING THROUGH

Importance of It. The complement of blocking is breaking through. Of the same importance that blocking is to the side acting on the offense, breaking through is to the side acting on the defense.

Of the two, it may fairly be claimed that breaking through is perhaps the more important, for in its highest development it is sufficient, barring accident, to prevent the opposing team from scoring, without which, of course, no game can ever be won.

Reason for This. On the other hand, weakness in breaking through is one of the surest signs of the inferiority of a team. The whole object in defensive play is to tackle the runner *behind his own line*, and this demands that the line of the opponent shall be broken through in less time than the ball can be advanced. It is not enough that the runner shall be stopped at the line.

It may sound paradoxical, but if he can reach the line, he can always gain a certain distance beyond it. It is an old adage that when the runner is allowed to reach the line before being tackled, he can always gain his five yards in three downs.

An Indication of Spirit. Perhaps there is no single feature in football which calls for a truer courage and stoutheartedness than breaking through the opponents' line. It is the carrying of the war into Africa; it is the invasion of the enemy's country; it shows the courage of the player in the indication which it gives of his spirit. The player who repeatedly tackles behind his opponents' line is the one who cannot wait for the opponent to come to him in his eagerness to get at his opponent. He is the player who plays from a love of the game, rather than from any desire for personal distinction.

It has often been advanced as one of the arguments against football, that a comparatively small number of players on a team really play from love of the game *per se*. It has been claimed that in a majority of cases there is some other motive at work, — love of college, desire for notoriety, pride, etc. However true or false this accusation may be, there are men who play football from love of the game, and they will be found tearing through the opponents' line the instant the ball is put in play.

Instructions to Guard and Tackle. The rules for breaking through are the same for any position or any player. It is true that a different importance attaches to the breaking through of different players, and that a greater responsibility for breaking through rests upon certain players, but the methods employed are substantially the same in every case.

If any player could be immediately pushed through the opponents' line, it is probable that the guard would be, of all men, the most destructive, for he might, by his prompt arrival, interfere with the passing of the quarter, which would be the instant jeopardizing of the enemy's entire movement, with the loss of at least a yard, and possibly the loss of the ball. It is to the tackle, however, and not to the guard, that we look for the greatest amount of breaking through the line. He should be rigidly required to go through the line on the defense. Any tendency on his part to wait until he can see where the run is to be made should be instantly suppressed.

When he is through the line he will be called upon to do one of two things, according as the play is directed toward his side of the line, or toward the opposite side. In the former case, his duty is to break up the interference, and if possible to secure the runner. In the latter case, his duty is to follow the runner, and bring him down from behind.

When not to go Through. Before beginning the explanation of the methods of breaking through, it may be well to point out the only case in which a green player, if he is a line man, should ever be coached *not* to break through, but to follow the play out behind his own line.

This one case is where he finds himself the third man from the end of the line, and some one of the opponents is stationed outside of that end rush. In such a case as this, upon being notified by the end rush that an opponent has gone outside of his position (or whether notified or not, in case he perceives the situation himself), he should, after retaining his position long enough to repel any attempt to pierce the line at that point, instantly go out behind his own line, and beyond his own end rush, and prepare to act as the end rush on any second pass of the ball to the man located on the outside of that end.

He must understand that the location of an opponent outside of his own end is always a menace, and, being the third man in the line, when any opponent has been placed beyond the limit of the end rush, responsibility for checking a play around that end devolves upon him. With this responsibility he is not freed, however, from a responsibility for his own position in the line; but with the placing of an opponent so far out from the centre, the probabilities strongly point to a double pass or a long pass, and the third man from the end of the line must be the man to get the runner, and not the end rush, whose duty it is to go straight for the first runner.

NOVEMBER 30, 1886. HARPER'S YOUNG PEOPLE.

A FOOT-BALL MATCH.

Discrimination between Players. With this single exception there is never a time when an inexperienced line man should be permitted to run back of his own line when acting on the defensive. It may be permitted sometimes to a veteran who thoroughly understands the game, and in whom this method of checking the advance of the opponents is not a careless tendency into which he has fallen through error. There are times in every game when a guard can most advantageously enter the defense by running back of his own line; but never should a guard be permitted to do this until he has demonstrated his ability to be trusted to act upon his own judgment, and to know instinctively when such times arrive.

Keep the Ball in Sight. From this slight digression we may now return to the subject proper, and discuss the

different methods of breaking through the line.

There are a variety of tactics which may be employed in breaking through. That one is always best which will work the quickest, and at the same time make it possible not to lose sight of the movement of the ball or the runner.

It is of much less advantage to be through the line, if in going through the player has lost sight of the movement or passing of the ball, and is, for the instant, uncertain which opponent is the runner. That instant's hesitation required to locate the ball is fatal for the success of his operations, for the situation changes so quickly that it is not safe to lose sight of the ball for a second.

Two Foundation Principles. The first rule, then, is to watch the ball, and go through the line with the ball. The

second rule is to keep yourself entirely free from the man opposite to you when going through, and prevent at all hazards any attempt on his part to hold or detain you. These

two maxims are always to be borne in mind when attempting to break through the opponents' line.

Best Position for the Body. The best position for breaking through is to keep about arm's length from your opponent. Make no movements unless they are made with some distinct intention. Remember that any motion on your part in any direction will naturally produce a similar motion on the part of your opponent; keep this thought in mind, and take advantage of it at every opportunity.

Importance of Quickness. In enumerating the methods of breaking through, let us first say that quickness is necessary for all of them. The position of the feet and the general inclination of the body should be the same as in blocking; but much more than in the case of blocking should the player be at  all times "on the edge." Watch the ball; try to detect, by any slightest indication, when and where it is going; break through with it if possible, and not a second later.

Attention to an Opponent. It is a safe rule to lay down that you can afford to almost ignore the man in front of you. With a little practice you can while watching the ball and never for a moment taking your eyes off it still see your opponent out of the corner of your eye. In other words, it is easily possible to bring your opponent and the ball both into the field of your vision at the same time. We have already said that you should keep at about arm's distance from your opponent,  but if possible this arm's distance should be in his territory, and not in yours.

Finally, go through with the arms well extended, so that they may be powerfully employed, to the end that you may not be bowled over by an interferer; and lastly, go through, circling on as small an arc as possible, to the end that your own line shall not be opened up too much.

Ten Methods of Breaking Through. (a) Strike your opponent on one side, as if making a feint to pass on that side, and dart quickly through on the other.

(b) Play for the outside arm of your opponent. You can sometimes catch this arm by a spring to one side. Your opponent, in the very attempt to free himself, may pull you through.

(c) Spring into your opponent with your arms extended, striking his chest a blow with both hands. The blow should be hard enough to start him back off his pins, or unsteady him, and you can then pass him on either side.

(d) The last method assumes that your opponent shall expose his chest. If he plays too low for this, see if it is not possible to take him by the head and pull him to one side or the other.

(e) Play very low yourself, with the body swung lightly backward, so that one hip is nearer the opponent than the other; let the arms be extended, and the hands opened out and together, nearly reaching the ground. The instant the ball is in play, with a sweeping upward stroke of the extended arms let your hands meet your opponent at about the height of his head. The force of the upward sweep will make the stroke strong enough to unsteady him, and perhaps make it possible for you to dart through.

(f) Catch your opponent by the shoulders and twist him around, taking care not to retain your hold upon him for more than an instant.

(g) Strike your opponent on the lower arm with both of your arms, imitating the swing of a sabre.

(h) With both hands and extended arms strike your opponent on either shoulder. That shoulder will either give way or push forward towards you. If it gives way, its righting power is instantly weakened, and you have the narrow side of his body opposing you, instead of the broad side. If, on the contrary, it advances to you, you will find that he has exposed his outer arm.

(i) Spring to one side, and with a sharp blow strike your opponent's arm down, and get through in that way.

(j) Decide which way you wish to go, then make any movement which will cause your opponent to move in the opposite direction to the one you have already decided upon. Let the feint be made the instant the ball goes, and your dodge will usually be successful.

Comments upon Them. We have given ten different methods of breaking through. All combined, however,

they are not as valuable as is the method of studying the man in front of you, noting his faults, and adapting your breaking through in such a way as to take advantage of them.

Vary your methods continually. Work out for yourself original methods of breaking through, and have a good number of them, for all occasions and different opponents. Above all, watch the ball, and never take your eyes off it for a moment.

Dangers of Scrapping when on the Defense. If your opponent takes trifling liberties with you, such as slapping your face, or undertaking to "play horse" with you in any way, remember that these digressions are merely made with a view to induce you to take your eyes off the ball and give your attention to him. Let all such actions merely determine you to a closer watch upon the ball. Your opportunity for repaying such attentions — if, indeed, they ever need to be repaid — will come when your positions are reversed. But make up your mind early in the season that no shouldering, scrapping, or horse-play of your opponent shall ever induce you to ignore or relax that keen attention upon the ball which is absolutely indispensable to the success of defensive work.

December 7, 1889.

BREAKING THROUGH A RUSH LINE.

Breaking Through on a Kick. The time when the opponents are about to kick is one of those critical moments when, by a single master stroke, the game may be won or lost. It is of the utmost importance that the kick should be blocked, or the kicker forced to have it down at the spot where he is standing. One such successful check will discourage your opponents more than a little, and the loss of the ground will be almost doubled in value by the loss of heart and spirit through the recognition of their own weakness at this vital stage.

For such occasions, therefore, you should reserve your very best efforts. If you have detected a certain weakness in your opponent which will permit you to break through him with comparative ease, hold it in reserve for the moment when the full-back retires for a kick. To break through at such a time is worth any three successful attempts in ordinary scrimmage plays. Apply your power quick and hard; summon all your strength for the crucial effort, and reach the kicker in the shortest possible space of time, springing high in the air, with uplifted arms, the moment you see that you arrive too late, and the kick is about to be effected. It is often possible, by thus leaping in the air, to intercept the ball, and do even greater injury to the opponents than if the kicker had been reached before he had the chance to get in his kick. For the blocked ball will probably rebound beyond the kicker, and your own side, charging forward, may easily gain possession of it and carry it down the field for a touch-down.

Formations which it is Unsafe to Break Through. In the old days, when heavy mass wedges were sometimes formed at a particular point in the line, the wisdom of breaking through was restricted, so far as the player was concerned at whose position the apex of the wedge was pointed. It was manifestly absurd to attempt to counteract by an onward plunge the combined force of the opposing mass. The player was, accordingly, coached to get as low as possible, even going down on his knees

FOOT-BALL—"COLLARED."

upon the ground, and to dive headlong between the feet of the oncoming players, and cause them to fall over his extended body. This was called "piling up the wedge;" and although it required a fearless player to make such an attack, it was one of the most common sights on the football field.

Of late years the use of such a heavy wedge has been effectually prevented by legislation, but the rules are still sufficiently elastic to make it possible for the formation of a body of men near a point in the line in such a manner that the attack may easily resolve itself into a solid wedge of a nature which it would be unwise to attempt to stop by permitting the player to go through the line in the ordinary way.

It would be well for the player to study this point, and watch for every appearance of such a formation. If the indications are strong for a mass play at his point in the line, his cue will be to get lower, and at all hazards prevent his opponent from lifting him up as a preliminary to pushing him back. The instant the ball is snapped, the play will resolve itself sufficiently for him to ascertain whether his premises were correct.

Should it prove to be a wedge or mass attack at his position, let him throw himself on the ground directly in front of it, and inclose in his outstretched arms all the feet and legs that he can seize; let him be especially careful, however, not to throw himself on the ground too soon, as, in that case, the wedge may easily avoid or step over him.

Above all, he must get very low to the ground, or he will surely be lifted up and carried along with the first onslaught of the impending mass.

Conclusion. It is impossible to close this chapter without emphasizing once more the vital importance of aggressiveness in this feature of defensive play. No more disheartening criticism can be made upon a team than to call attention to the fact that they invariably make their tackles after the opponents have reached and pierced the line. A courageous and aggressive policy of breaking through is one of the most hopeful indications in a team.

It is the more difficult to inculcate this style of play, because the excuse is always ready that the play may be coming at the exact point in the line at which the player is standing. There is, of course, in all such cases, a double responsibility, — the responsibility of protecting his own hole, and of breaking through and meeting the runner.

But while these are two separate responsibilities, they can never be separated in their consideration. They really belong together. Each one is the true accompaniment of the other. Let the player never hesitate or hold back from any notion that the play may be coming at his place in the line.

Rather let him be encouraged to go through "on the jump," with his eyes wide open, with attention never for a moment distracted from the ball, and with his arms sufficiently extended to enable him to meet and resist an oncoming interference.

By such tactics he may at times overrun his man; but this is a hopeful fault, compared with the weakness or laxity which holds him back and permits him to meet the runner at the line rather than tackle him in his own territory.

TACKLING A RUNNER.

THE LINEMEN IN TEAM PLAY

Defensive Team Play. Defensive team play should be begun by instructing some pair of men to help each other out in word and act. For example, take the guard and tackle. Tell each separately the strength and weakness of the other, and then explain how they must aid one another by supplemental work. If they have good heads they will take it up readily.

There should be no loud calling out of what the opponents are likely to do. That sort of work often does more harm than good. But a general caution, such as "Look out for a fake!" or something of that kind, is all right.

Especially should the two men learn that they are responsible for *results*, — not merely for their acts, but what comes from those acts! This brings about unselfish team play and does away with the host of excuses.

LIST OF ILLUSTRATIONS

AMERICAN FOOTBALL, by Walter Camp, 1891

A SCIENTIFIC AND PRACTICAL TREATISE ON
AMERICAN FOOTBALL FOR SCHOOLS AND COLLEGES,
By A. A. Stagg and Henry L. Williams, 1893

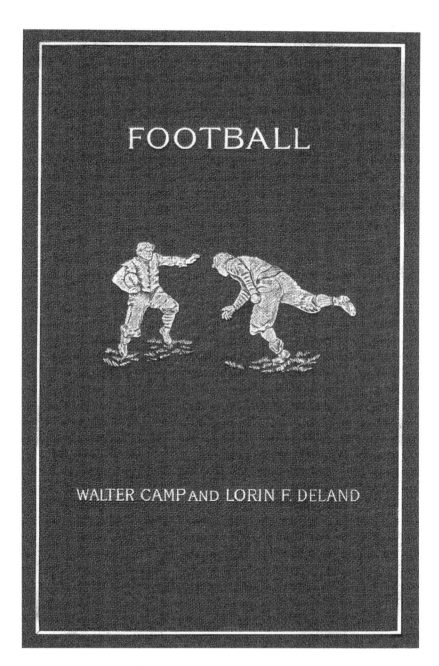

FOOTBALL, by Walter Camp and Lorin F. Deland, 1896

THE GAME in the 1890s

DIFFERENCES FROM TODAY:
- 110 yard field
- 3 downs to gain 5 yards
- No forward passing
- Ball was watermelon-shaped
- Same 11 played offense, defense, and special teams
- Full-back was also the defensive safety and kicker
- Substituted players could not reenter the game
- Scrimmage kicks could be recovered by either team
- Sideline coaching was not permitted during a game
- Scoring values: TD-4, PAT-2, FG-5, SAFETY-2
- All players wore pads but none wore helmets

FROM 1891 TO 1896:
- The sport was under attack for its brutality
- Flying Wedge was invented, deployed, and prohibited
- Number of players moving at snap lowered from ten to one
- Officials blew whistles to end plays
- Unnecessary roughness and piling-on became penalties
- Stagg's Chicago team huddled versus Michigan in 1896

STREAMLINED SINCE:
- Point-After-Touchdown procedure
- Sideline inbounds, with hash marks
- Signals, with the huddle
- The shape of the ball, for passing

MODERN TRANSLATIONS:
- Rusher or forward = Lineman
- Rush line back = Linebacker
- In touch = Out of bounds
- Fair ("from a fair") = Put ball in play from out of bounds
- Interference = Run blocking, not the modern penalty

9174740R0

Made in the USA
Charleston, SC
17 August 2011